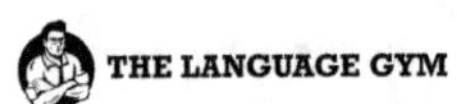
THE LANGUAGE GYM

SPANISH GCSE REVISION

ANSWER BOOK

ENVIRONMENT, HEALTH & CAREERS

THE LANGUAGE GYM

TABLE OF CONTENTS

Unit 1. Food and eating out

1. Match up
Hoy – Today   **Esta mañana** – This morning   **Esta tarde** – This evening
Me gustaría comprar – I would like to buy   **El queso** – Cheese   **Muy sabroso** – Very tasty
No soporto – I can't stand   **La carne** – Meat   **Demasiado picante** – Too spicy
Un vaso de agua – A glass of water

2. Gapped translation
a. Quisiéramos **pedir** un café   b. Me gustaría **comprar** patatas fritas   c. Para la **cena** como **comida** caliente
d. Lo que me gusta **comer** es el **queso**   e. Lo que **odio** son los **refrescos**
f. Lo que **menos** me gustan son las **verduras**

3. Positive or negative
a. Positive   b. Negative   c. Negative   d. Positive   e. Negative   f. Positive   g. Positive   h. Negative   i. Positive
j. Positive

4. Faulty translation
a. For **breakfast**   b. **Vegetables**   c. What I like the **least**   d. My favourite **dish**   e. **Quite/rather** delicious
f. **Very** nutritious   g. I drink a glass of **water**   h. What I **hate**   i. **Fizzy drinks**   j. **Very salty**

5. Sentence puzzle
a. Lo que me encanta comer es el pan   b. Lo que menos me gusta son las verduras
c. Lo que no como es la comida frita   d. Porque es demasiado grasiento   e. Lo que no soporto son los mariscos
f. Bebo chocolate caliente   g. Tomo un vaso de agua   h. Tomo un plato caliente   i. Me gustaría beber un café
j. Para la cena como tortilla española   k. Porque es muy saludable

6. Translate into English
a. What I hate is coffee   b. I would like to buy fruit   c. We would like to eat fish
d. What I like eating the most is bread   e. I love drinking hot chocolate   f. For dinner I have a hot meal
g. What I prefer eating is cheese   h. Because they are tasteless   i. Because it is delicious and nutritious

7. Broken sentences
a. Para la merienda bebo un chocolate caliente   b. Para el desayuno me gustaría tomar un café
c. Hoy me gustaría comer fabada asturiana   d. Lo que menos me gusta es el queso
e. Mi plato favorito es el gazpacho andaluz   f. Lo que odio comer son los mariscos
g. A mediodía tomo fruta   h. Quisiéramos pedir gambas al pil pil

8. Gapped translation
a. Esta **tarde**   b. Nos gustaría **pedir**   c. Chocolate **caliente**   d. **Bebo** un **vaso** de agua   e. Quisiera **comer** fruta
f. Un **plato** caliente   g. Los **refrescos**

9. True or false
a. True   b. True   c. True   d. False   e. False   f. True   g. True

10. Complete with the correct verb
a. Quisiéramos **tomar** un café   b. Para comer **tomo** pollo con arroz   c. Mi comida favorita **es** pan con queso
d. Lo que no me **gusta** es comer pescado   e. Lo que no **soporto** son las verduras
f. Para la merienda **bebo** un chocolate caliente   g. Esta mañana me **gustaría** desayunar fruta
h. Lo que **odio** son los refrescos   i. Hoy **quisiera** comer carne

11. Translate into Spanish
a. **G**ambas   b. **B**astante   c. **S**aludable   d. **V**erduras   e. **Q**ueso   f. **S**abroso   g. **P**ollo   h. **N**utritivo
i. **P**escado   j. **M**añana   k. **R**ealmente   l. **C**omida frita

12. Choose the correct translation
a. This evening   b. Meat   c. I drink   d. Healthy   e. Tasty   f. Too greasy   g. Nutritious
h. My favourite dish   i. Very sweet   j. For breakfast

13. Guided translation
a. Lo que más me gusta es el queso   b. Mi comida favorita   c. Prefiero comer un plato caliente
d. Mi plato favorito es arroz con leche   e. Lo que odio son los refrescos
f. Para el almuerzo tomo pollo con arroz   g. Bebo un vaso de agua   h. Quisiera comer carne

14. Translate into Spanish
a. A mediodía quisiera/me gustaría comer carne con patatas fritas
b. Hoy quisiera/me gustaría tomar un café con mi amigo/a y después me gustaría comprar fruta
c. Para el almuerzo, normalmente como pollo con arroz y bebo un vaso de agua
d. Lo que me gusta comer es el queso porque es delicioso
e. Lo que prefiero comer es el pescado porque es saludable y sabroso
f. Para el desayuno como pan y queso y bebo (un) café
g. Para la cena como un plato caliente. Me gusta comer carne y verduras
h. Para la merienda normalmente tomo un chocolate caliente o café y como pan con mantequilla
i. Lo que me encanta comer es el chocolate porque es dulce y delicioso
j. Lo que odio comer son las gambas al pil pil porque son muy picantes y demasiado saladas

15. Find the Spanish equivalent in the text
a. hoy   b. compraré   c. pollo   d. agua mineral   e. un plato caliente   f. verduras   g. tomaré
h. es bueno/a para la salud

16. Faulty translation
In general, I eat a **lot** for breakfast. I take **two pieces** of toast with butter and jam **or honey** and I also **eat a yoghurt with banana** and cereals. Also, I drink a cup of coffee and a glass of **orange** juice. I know **it is a lot,** but for me, breakfast is the **most** important meal of the day.

17. Complete the sentences
a. I love **cheese** because it's **very tasty** and **healthy,** as long as you eat it in **moderation**
b. I also like eating **bread** very much because it is **nutritious** and it's a part of the Mediterranean diet
c. My favourite **dish** is Asturian bean stew because it's **really exquisite** and my mother **cooks** it to **perfection**
d. My **favourite** dessert is *crème brûlée* because it's so **sweet** and **delicious**!

18. Translate into English
a. On the other hand   b. I hate eating   c. It was too disgusting   d. I also can't stand
e. I'm allergic to nuts   f. All over the place / everywhere   g. Never again

19. True, false or not mentioned
a. False   b. True   c. False   d. False   e. False   f. True   g. Not mentioned   h. True

20. Compete the text
Hoy al mediodía me **encantaría** ir al restaurante porque es el cumpleaños de mi hermana y siempre lo **celebramos** en familia. Como entrantes, me gustaría comer **verduras** crudas porque son ligeras y **saludables.** Luego me gustaría tomar carne y patatas fritas como plato principal porque la carne es sabrosa y nutritiva. De postre me gustaría comer arroz con leche y para **beber** probablemente un zumo o agua mineral.
Mi comida favorita del día es la **cena** y normalmente como mucho por la noche. A menudo como **pollo** con arroz o pasta con salsa de tomate, todo acompañado por verduras ecológicas del huerto de mi **abuelo.** Tenemos suerte porque siempre están **frescas** y sabemos que no tienen pesticidas ni fertilizantes **químicos.**

21. True or false
a. True   b. False   c. False   d. False   e. False   f. True   g. True   h. False

22. Match up
Lo que me encanta – What I love   **Los dulces** – Sweets   **Es malo** – It's bad   **Para la salud** – For your health
¡Qué lujo! – What a treat   **No puedo** – I can't   **Voy a comprar** – I am going to buy
Para toda mi familia – For my whole family   **En cambio** – On the other hand   **Lo que odio** – What I hate
Bastante salado – Quite salty

23. Answer the questions

a. She loves eating chocolate and desserts   b. Her favourite desserts are French toast and doughnuts
c. Every Sunday morning she buys churros with chocolate at the market place
d. The dish she finds too spicy is spicy prawns   e. Tere finds seafood quite salty
f. She hates fried food because it is too greasy

24. Translate into Spanish

a. Sé que es malo para la salud   b. Es tan bueno que no me puedo resistir   c. Cada domingo por la mañana
d. Es demasiado picante para mí   e. No me gustan los mariscos   f. Prefiero comida dulce
g. No soporto los refrescos

25. Translate the paragraph

En general, como muy poco para el desayuno. Solo tomo una tostada con mermelada o mantequilla y, a veces, también como un plátano. De bebida caliente bebo una taza de té con azucar y, a veces, también bebo un vaso de zumo de naranja. Creo que es suficiente para mí. El desayuno es la comida más importante del día.

26. Complete with an appropriate word

a. Quisiera **comer** carne esta noche   b. Es **tan** bueno que no lo puedo resistir
c. Lo que odio son las **gambas** al pil pil   d. Lo que más me gusta **comer** es el chocolate
e. Mi comida **favorita** es la cena   f. Lo **que** prefiero comer son los mariscos
g. Sé que es **malo** para la salud, pero me encanta   h. Bebo una **taza** de café y un **vaso** de zumo
i. **Lo que** no soporto es la comida frita porque es grasienta
j. Mi **plato** favorito es pescado con patatas y verduras   k. Me encanta la fruta **porque** es sana y deliciosa

27. Translate into Spanish

a. Para el almuerzo normalmente como pollo con arroz y bebo un vaso de agua mineral
b. Lo que me encanta comer es pan porque es sabroso y saludable
c. Lo que prefiero comer es el pescado porque es salado
d. Lo que no me gusta comer es la comida frita porque es muy grasienta
e. No soporto los refrescos porque en mi opinión son demasiado dulces
f. No me gusta la fabada asturiana porque es demasiado salada para mí.

28. Write a 140-word composition

Free writing

Unit 2. Healthy/unhealthy living

1. Choose the correct translation
a. Good health   b. Usually   c. To sleep   d. Healthy   e. I will try   f. Spinach   g. I think that
h. A balanced diet   i. Organic food   j. To quit smoking

2. Match up
Los huevos – Eggs   **Bebo** – I drink   **Pienso que** – I think that   **Debería evitar** – I should avoid
Productos frescos – Fresh products   **Intentaré** – I will try   **Beber alcohol** – To drink alcohol
Evitar fumar – To avoid smoking   **Mejorar** – To improve   **Todos los días** – Every day
Cocinar yo mismo – To cook myself   **Debo dejar de** – I must quit

3. Complete with the correct option
a. Para tener energía hay que comer **sano**   b. Hay que **dormir** ocho horas cada noche
c. **Hago** ejercicio regularmente   d. **Debería** comer más verduras   e. Tengo una dieta **equilibrada**
f. Creo que **estoy** en forma   g. Intentaré comer **menos** dulces   h. Debo **dejar** de fumar

4. Sentence puzzle
a. Intento dormir ocho horas cada noche
b. Me gustan bastante las naranjas porque son ricas en vitaminas
c. Voy a hacer un esfuerzo para comer menos dules
d. Tengo la impresión de que sigo una dieta equilibrada porque como de todo
e. Creo que estoy en forma porque como comida ecológica
f. Si tuviera más tiempo cocinaría más yo mismo

5. Translate into English
a. To be in shape   b. I try to sleep eight hours every night   c. Eggs are rich in protein
d. Generally I drink a lot of water   e. I eat a lot of vegetables and a bit of fruit
f. If I could I would cook myself   g. I will try to eat fewer sweets   h. I should stop drinking alcohol
i. I should also avoid smoking   j. I will make an effort to eat more healthy
k. I'm in good shape because I eat everything   l. I believe I have a healthy diet
m. If I had more time I would exercise more   n. I think I follow a balanced diet

6. True or false
a. False   b. True   c. False   d. False   e. True   f. True

7. Spot and supply the one missing word in each sentence
a. Hago un esfuerzo para **comer** más verduras
b. Para estar en forma intento dormir **ocho** horas cada noche
c. Creo que sigo una dieta equilibrada porque como de **todo**
d. Me encantan los huevos porque son **ricos** en vitaminas y proteínas
e. **Por** lo general bebo mucha agua en el desayuno

8. Anagrams
a. Normalmente   b. Mejorar   c. Ecológica   d. Dieta   e. Equilibrado   f. Dormir   g. Verduras   h. Dulces
i. Cocinar

9. Complete as appropiate
a. Si **tuviera** tiempo cocinaría yo mismo   b. **Debería** dejar de beber alcohol
c. Voy a hacer un **esfuerzo** para comer más verduras   d. Para estar en forma debería **dejar** de fumar
e. Me encantan las espinacas porque son ricas en **vitaminas**
f. Para tener más **energía** es importante comer sano   g. Para estar en forma **hago** ejercicio regularmente
h. **Intentaré** comer menos dulces   i. Si pudiera cocinaría más a **menudo**

10. Correct spelling errors

a. Pienso que   b. Una dieta equilibrada   c. Para mejorar la salud   d. Comer sano   e. Si tuviera más tiempo
f. Para estar en forma   g. Intentaré   h. Beber alcohol   i. Todos los días   j. Si pudiera

11. Complete with the missing word

a. **Para** tener buena salud hay que comer de todo   b. **Por** lo general bebo té con azúcar
c. Es necesario hacer ejercicio y beber **mucha** agua   d. Sigo **una** dieta equilibrada y no fumo
e. Debería dejar **de** fumar   f. Intentaré beber **menos** alcohol   g. Es muy malo **para** ti
h. A **menudo** como espinacas y bebo café   i. Las naranjas son ricas **en** vitaminas
j. Llevo una dieta sana y como **productos** frescos

12. Complete the words

a. Mejorar   b. Sano   c. Esfuerzo   d. Ecológica   e. Regularmente   f. Minerales   g. Productos
h. A menudo   i. Bastante   j. Equilibrado

13. Tangled translation

a. Para tener buena **salud**, hay que tener una dieta **equilibrada** y **dormir** ocho **horas** cada **noche**
b. **Pienso** que **sigo** una dieta equilibrada **porque** yo **como** muchos productos **frescos**
c. **En** el futuro voy a **hacer** un esfuerzo para comer **menos dulces**
d. **Desde ahora**, intentaré comer **más verduras** y **beber** menos **alcohol**
e. También **debería dejar** de **fumar** porque es **malo** para la salud
f. Pienso **que** tengo una **dieta** sana **porque** como de **todo**
g. Si **tuviera** más tiempo, **cocinaría** más **a menudo**
h. **Si pudiera**, cocinaría más **yo mismo**

14. Translate into Spanish

a. Intento comer menos dulces y más verduras
b. Me gustan bastante las naranjas porque son ricas en vitaminas
c. Creo que estoy en forma porque hago deporte cada día
d. Para tener energía intento dormir ocho horas cada noche
e. Si tuviera más tiempo haría el esfuerzo de cocinar más yo mismo
f. Para estar en mejor forma debería evitar fumar
g. En el futuro haré un esfuerzo para comer más fruta
h. Si tuviera más tiempo cocinaría más a menudo

15. Find the Spanish equivalent

a. El sueño es tan importante como la dieta   b. Hago ejercicio tres veces por semana
c. Me permite eliminar el estrés   d. Bebo mucha agua   e. Soy vegetariano desde hace tres años
f. Antes comía mucha carne y comida frita   g. Desde que lo dejé   h. También perdí peso
i. Ahora me siento mejor conmigo mismo   j. Tengo la impresión de que llevo una dieta equilibrada
k. Como una amplia variedad de alimentos frescos   l. No son saludables
m. Todavía como un poco de comida basura   n. Refrescos   o. Contienen demasiada azúcar

16. Complete the translation

I think I follow a **balanced** diet because I eat a wide variety of **fresh** foods every day and I don't **eat** pre-cooked foods like **before**. Pre-cooked foods are generally high in **salt** and fat, and therefore **unhealthy**. Although I prefer **homemade** food, I must **admit** that I still eat a bit of **junk** food from time to time, like French fries with **mayonnaise**.

17. Answer the following questions

a. Sergio exercises three times a week, sleeps eight hours every night and follows a healthy and balanced diet.
b. He says that sleep is as important to our health as a good diet.
c. He exercises three times a week.
d. He feels much better in his own skin, he has lost weight, he has more energy and is in better shape.
e. *Comida casera* means homemade food.
f. Sergio wants to eat fewer sweets and he will try to drink fewer fizzy drinks.
g. He says he should avoid drinking alcohol and smoking cigarettes on Saturdays.

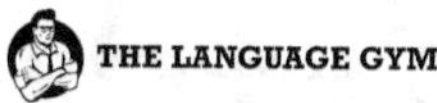

18. Complete the sentences
a. Every week, Lucía trains **twice a week** with her **football** club
b. As for food, she tries to eat with **moderation**
c. She **always** drinks a lot of **water**, around **two** litres per **day**
d. She particularly loves **spinach** because it's rich in **vitamins** and **minerals** and **eggs** because they are rich in protein
e. She also likes **meat**, but she **tries** to eat it only **once** or **twice** per **week**
f. To have energy, she drinks **fresh fruit juices** and she tries to **sleep** at least **eight** hours every **night** because otherwise she is **tired** and in a **bad** mood
g. Moreover, she **buys** organic food and she **cooks** at home, so she knows **exactly** what is on her plate
h. She loves cooking and she would like to **become** a **famous** chef one day and **open** her **own** restaurant
i. To keep her good **health** she **doesn't** drink alcohol nor **smoke** when she sees her friends at the weekend
j. However, she should also **stop** eating so many **sweets** because they contain a lot of **sugar**

19. True, false or not mentioned
a. False b. True c. Not mentioned d. True e. True f. Not mentioned g. True h. False

20. Verb quiz
a. I train b. I try c. I drink d. I believe that e. I eat f. I sleep g. I must stop h. To maintain

21. Translate into English
a. To be healthy b. It is necessary to exercise regularly c. I train twice a week d. I think I do enough sport
e. I try to eat with moderation f. Normally I drink a lot of water g. I try to sleep at least eight hours every night
h. I'm tired i. I'm in a bad mood j. I have a healthy diet k. I know exactly what is on my plate
l. I prepare food for my whole family m. I would love to open my own restaurant
n. I have to stop eating so many sweets

22. Correct the spelling and grammar errors
a. Bebo mucha agua b. También me **gusta** comer carne c. Creo que tengo una dieta equilibrada
d. Soy **yo** quien suele preparar las comidas e. Intentaré comer menos dulces f. Es bueno **para** la salud
g. Debería beber menos alco**hol** h. Son ricos en miner**ales** i. Me encanta **cocinar** y usar productos frescos
j. Debo dejar de fumar **porque** no es sano k. Para **estar** en forma hay que comer sano

23. Gapped translation
a. Los **refrescos** b. Menos **dulces** c. **Dejar** de fumar d. **Dormir** suficiente e. Comida **ecológica**
f. Comida **casera** g. **Solamente** una vez por semana h. **Evitar** beber i. Una dieta **equilibrada**
j. De **vez** en **cuando** k. Dos **veces** por semana

24. Translate into Spanish
Para estar en forma intento comer sano todos los días. Para el desayuno, como pan y dos huevos y bebo chocolate caliente. De vez en cuando también bebo un zumo de fruta fresca.
Para el almuerzo, como una comida caliente, normalmente pollo y arroz, y bebo un poco de agua. Me encanta el pollo porque es saludable y sabroso.
Para estar en forma es importante hacer ejercicio regularmente. Personalmente, entreno dos veces por semana con mi club de fútbol y también tengo un partido todos los fines de semana.
Para mejorar mi salud debería evitar fumar y beber alcohol cuando salgo con mis amigos. En el futuro intentaré comer menos dulces y voy a hacer un esfuerzo para comer más verduras.
Finalmente, si tuviera más tiempo, cocinaría más a menudo porque es más sano/saludable y, en general, más delicioso también. Debería dormir ocho horas cada noche para estar menos cansado.

25. Write a 140-word composition
Free writing

Unit 3. Young people and fashion

1. Match up
Actualmente – Currently   **La ropa** – Clothes   **Hoy en día** – Nowadays   **La moda** – Fashion
Las joyas – Jewellery   **Una forma de** – A way to   **Los tatuajes** – Tattoos   **Presión** – Pressure
La imagen – The look   **La tendencia** – Trend   **Llevar** – To wear

2. Complete with the correct verb
a. La moda puede **llevar** a la exclusión   b. Es necesario **animar** a los jóvenes a desarrollar su propio estilo
c. La ropa **permite** definir la identidad   d. Los accesorios ayudan a **diferenciarse** de los demás
e. Ser **diferente** puede llevar al acoso   f. La forma de vestir es una manera de **expresarse**
g. El estilo permite **atraer** a las chicas   h. La mayoría de los adolescentes **lleva** ropa de marca

3. Gapped translation
a. Clothes **help** one to improve one's image   b. Accessories **help** develop one's identity
c. **Tattoos** help stand out from the **others**   d. We must encourage **young people** to experiment
e. Personally, I love all the latest **trends**   f. We **must** encourage young people to **develop** their own look

4. Broken words
a. **Los demás**   b. Actualmente   c. Lo triste es   d. Las últimas tendencias   e. La ropa de marca
f. Mucha gente joven   g. Llevar a la exclusión   h. La forma de vestir   i. Los tatuajes   j. Personalmente
k. Las joyas

5. Faulty translation
a. The **sad** thing is   b. I **love** fashion   c. To lead to **bullying**   d. **Current** trends   e. **Lots of** young people   f. √
g. To **wear** jewellery   h. √   i. **Nowadays**   j. To **give** the opportunity

6. Choose the correct option
a. llevar a   b. dan   c. integrarse   d. al   e. me   f. en / ropa   g. a   h. animar   i. demás

7. Find the Spanish
a. Es necesario   b. Para expresarse   c. Lo triste es   d. Poner presión   e. Inspirarse   f. Hoy en día
g. La apariencia   h. La moda   i. La ropa   j. Los jóvenes

8. Match the words/phrases
Triste – **Desafortunado**   Los jóvenes – **Los adolescentes**   Debemos – **Es necesario**   La mayoría – **Muchos**
Ayudan – **Permiten**   El estilo – **La forma de vestir**   Me gusta – **Me encanta**   Hacerse notar – **Atraer**
Expresar – **Mostrar**   Hoy en día – **Actualmente**

9. Sentence puzzle
a. Mucha gente joven lleva ropa de marca   b. A veces la moda puede llevar a la exclusión
c. Los tatuajes permiten diferenciarse de los demás   d. Mucha gente joven se viste para causar buen impresión
e. Las joyas ayudan a mejorar la imagen   f. Personalmente suelo inspirarme en las últimas tendencias
g. Debemos animar a los jóvenes a experimentar   h. La moda es una forma de hacerse notar
i. Debo decir que me encanta inspirarme en los *influencers* de Instagram

10. Choose the correct translation
a. The sad thing is   b. Currently   c. Nowadays   d. To improve one's image   e. Branded clothes
f. The latest trends   g. Most   h. To lead to exclusion   i. To improve one's image   j. It is necessary

11. Spot and supply the missing word
a. Hoy **en** día los jóvenes se inspiran en la moda   b. La apariencia es **una** forma de expresarse
c. La ropa da la oportunidad **de** definir la identidad   d. Lo triste es **que** ser diferente puede llevar al acoso
e. Es necesario permitir **a** los adolescentes desarrollar su estilo
f. Me encanta inspirarme **en** los *influencers* de Instagram
g. Debo decir que me gustan **las** últimas tendencias   h. Los tatuajes permiten **a** diferenciarse de demás

12. Translate into Spanish
a. Los tatuajes ayudan a diferenciarse de los demas   b. Lo desafortunado es
c. Debemos permitir a los jóvenes desarrollar su propia imagen   d. Es necesario
e. Desde mi punto de vista   f. Debo decir que me encantan las últimas tendencias
g. La moda nos anima a malgastar dinero   h. Los jóvenes se visten para hacerse notar

13. Complete with a suitable word
a. Las prendas de **ropa** ayudan a **mejorar** la imagen
b. Actualmente, la **mayoría** de los adolescentes desarrolla su **propio** estilo
c. La **forma** de vestir es una manera de **integrarse** en el grupo
d. Es **necesario** animar a los jóvenes experimentar con diferentes **estilos**
e. Lo triste **es** que la moda puede **llevar** a la **exclusión**
f. Las joyas **dan** la oportunidad de **definir** la identidad
g. **Hoy** en día muchos adolescentes **llevan** ropa barata y **cómoda**
h. Personalmente, me **gusta** mucho experimentar con diferentes **estilos**
i. Debo **decir** que ser diferente da la oportunidad de **hacerse** notar

14. Find the Spanish equivalent in the text
a. Accesorios   b. Estilo   c. Su   d. Vestir   e. Se ha convertido   f. Hoy   g. Ropa   h. Una manera de   i. Joyas
j. Importante   k. Marcas   l. Joven   m. Demostrarlo   n. Ya   o. Más   p. Maquillaje

15. Complete the translation
I think it is **important** to encourage teenagers to **express themselves**. They must be allowed to **experiment** with different fashion **styles** because in the future they will **be able** to define their own identity. To be **up to date** and know the latest trends, some young people get **inspired** by Instagram influencers.

16. Faulty translation
Clothes, accessories, **jewelery** and tattoos **give** you the opportunity to **personalise** your image and get noticed on the **street**. I must say that I **love** seeing someone **wearing** clothes in a different way that shows their **individual** style. I **personally** love to wear **vintage** clothing, especially from the 1950s.

17. Translate into English
a. I must say   b. A lot of young people   c. Bullying   d. More and more   e. Dress style   f. The others
g. Nowadays   h. Makeup   i. Latest trends   j. Own style   k. They feel obliged   l. To personalise   m. Especially
n. Get noticed

18. Complete the following sentences and then translate them into English
a. No les **importa** sacrificarse: They don't mind to make a sacrifice
b. Cambia **constantemente**: Changes constantly   c. **Son** los detalles que: It's the details that
d. El uso de colores y **telas**: The use of colours and fabrics
e. La mezcla de **muchos** estilos: The mix of many styles   f. Los **adolescentes** que conozco: Teenagers I know
g. Las modas se **repiten**: Fashion repeats   h. Hoy en **día** en las **calles**: Nowadays on the streets
i. Las que **llevaban** nuestros padres: The ones that our parents wore

19. Complete the sentences based on paragraphs 3 and 4
a. Accessories and **jewelery** help create a personal **style** to stand out from the **others**
b. In the same **way**, clothing and tattoos **give** you the opportunity to **express** yourself without words
c. We have to **support** young people to **experiment** with different **styles**
d. The **sad** thing is that it can lead to **exclusion**
e. **First** of all, not everyone can **afford** expensive clothes and **accessories**
f. Secondly, some teenagers are simply not **interested** in **fashion**

20. Find the Spanish equivalent in the text
a. Ignorar   b. Ropa   c. Jóvenes   d. Diseño   e. Tela   f. Cómoda   g. Simplemente   h. Manera
i. Compañeros   j. Presión

21. True or false
a. False   b. False   c. True   d. True   e. False

THE LANGUAGE GYM

22. Complete with the options below
A **veces** parece que la ropa que llevan los jóvenes no es muy **cómoda**, pero en mi opinión no les **importa** sacrificarse un poco para **integrarse** en un grupo y atraer a las chicas o chicos.
La moda **cambia** constantemente, pero realmente muchos **diseños** de ropa que vemos hoy en día en las calles son prendas basadas en las que llevaban nuestros padres o **incluso** abuelos. Son los detalles lo que hacen los diseños **más** modernos, por ejemplo, la **mezcla** de distintos estilos o el uso de colores y telas de manera que nunca se ha hecho antes (como materiales de plástico fluorescentes o transparentes).
Desafortunadamente, la moda también tiene **aspectos** negativos que no debemos ignorar. Lo triste es **que** puede llevar a la exclusión, y no todo el mundo puede **permitirse** ropa y accesorios caros.

23. Tiled translation
Los accesorios y las joyas ayudan a definir la imagen y crean un estilo personal para diferenciarse de los demás. De la misma manera, la ropa y los tatuajes te dan la oportunidad de expresarte sin palabras. Debemos apoyar a los jóvenes a experimentar con diferentes estilos y permitirles desarrollar su propia forma de vestir.
Desafortunadamente, la moda también tiene aspectos negativos que no debemos ignorar. Lo triste es que puede llevar a la exclusión. Algunos adolescentes simplemente no están interesados en la moda, pero la presión de sus compañeros sigue ahí y pueden sufrir acoso.

24. Split phrases
a. Las joyas y accesorios ayudan a **definir la identidad y mejorar la imagen**
b. Algunos de los adolescentes simplemente **no están interesados en las últimas tendencias**
c. Desafortunadamente, ser diferente **puede llevar al acoso y a la exclusión**
d. A veces parece que **la ropa que llevan no es muy cómoda**
e. Personalmente me encanta seguir las **nuevas tendencias a través de Instagram**
f. Creo que las prendas de ropa ayudan **a definir el estilo personal**
g. Hoy en día muchos jóvenes **llevan ropa de marca y a menudo bastante cara**
h. Los tatuajes son una **de las formas para definir la identidad**
i. La moda también tiene aspectos **negativos que no debemos ignorar**

25. Translate into Spanish
a. El estilo de vestir es una manera de expresarse
b. Hoy en día muchos jóvenes llevan ropa de marca
c. Debemos dejar que los adolescentes desarrollen su propio estilo
d. Desafortunadamente, la moda también tiene aspectos negativos
e. Algunos adolescentes no pueden permitirse ropa cara
f. Hay jóvenes que simplemente no están interesados en la moda
g. Me gustan mucho las últimas tendencias
h. Desafortunadamente, a veces ser diferente puede llevar a la exclusión

26. Translate into Spanish
A la mayoría de los jóvenes les gusta la moda y las últimas tendencias. Para ellos es una manera de expresarse y definir su identidad.
Por lo general, llevan ropa de marca y les encantan las zapatillas de moda. Ademas, a menudo tienen tatuajes, joyas o complementos para diferenciarse de los demás creando su propio estilo.
Desafortunadamente, la moda puede fomentar las burlas y llevar a la exclusión. En primer lugar, algunos adolescentes no pueden permitirse ropa cara para estar al día, y en segundo lugar, algunos adolescentes no están interesados en la moda, pero la presión de sus compañeros sigue ahí.
Lo triste es que esto puede llevar al acoso y a ser excluído del grupo.

27. Write a 140-word text
Free writing

Unit 4. Environment: global problems

1. Match up
El paisaje – Landscape **El nivel del mar** – The sea level **Un desafío fundamental** – A fundamental challenge
La escasez – Shortage **Poner en peligro** – To endanger **La inundación** – Flood
El sobreconsumo – Overconsumption **El efecto invernadero** – The greenhouse effect **La huella** – Footprint
Amenazar – To threaten **El desperdicio** – Waste

2. Complete the words and translate them into English
a. Desafío: Challenge b. Diversidad: Diversity c. Aumento: Increase d. Escasez: Shortage
e. Contaminación: Pollution f. Una gran influencia: A big influence g. El ser humano: Human being
h. Especies vegetales: Vegetal species i. El deshielo de los polos: The melting of the ice caps
j. Las inundaciones: Floods

3. Sentence puzzle
a. La contaminación del agua b. El aumento de la población c. En la playa d. El deshielo de los polos
e. La subida del nivel del mar f. En las zonas costeras g. El desperdicio de alimentos
h. La diversidad de la fauna i. La escasez de alimentos j. El calentamiento global

4. Anagrams
a. Paisaje b. Agotamiento c. Catástrofes d. Inundaciones e. Calentamiento f. Escasez
g. Sobreconsumo h. Aumento i. Huella j. Extinción

5. Gapped translation
a. The **extinction** of plant species b. The population **increase** c. The **loss** of biodiversity
d. The **melting** of the ice caps e. **Soil** pollution f. The human **being** g. A universal **problem**

6. Break the flow
a. El agotamiento de los recursos b. Está dejando una huella c. La temperatura de los océanos
d. La subida del nivel del mar e. Juega un papel importante f. Tiene una gran influencia
g. Los desastres naturales

7. Complete with the options below
a. La población **mundial** no para de aumentar cada año
b. El **sobreconsumo** tiene una gran influencia en la escasez de alimentos
c. El efecto invernadero se acelera por la **contaminación**
d. La subida del nivel del mar **provoca** inundaciones
e. La pérdida de la **biodiversidad** es un problema universal
f. El **desperdicio** provoca el agotamiento de los **recursos** naturales
g. El ser **humano** está dejando una huella cada vez mayor en el paisaje
h. La contaminación del **aire**, del agua y del suelo se ha convertido en un desafío **fundamental**

8. Missing letter challenge
a. Un papel importante b. Los desastres naturales c. El ser humano d. La población mundial
e. Las especies animales f. El nivel del mar g. La biodiversidad h. Los recursos naturales
i. El paisaje j. Las zonas costeras k. El medio ambiente l. Un desafío fundamental

9. Faulty translation
a. Water pollution is a universal **problem** b. The exhaustion of resources **has become** a challenge for humanity
c. The greenhouse effect is **accelerated** by pollution d. The sea level rise causes **floods**
e. The world population doesn't stop **increasing** f. The ocean temperature keeps going **up**
g. The melting of the ice caps **causes** floods

10. Translate into English
a. The air pollution b. The extinction of animal species c. The melting of the ice caps d. Food waste
e. It is leaving a mark f. In coastal areas g. Plays an important role h. In the environment
i. The diversity of flora j. Human being k. Every time bigger l. It has become m. It doesn't stop growing

n. The loss of biodiversity   o. Global warming   p. The overconsumption   q. Natural disasters
r. Human activity   s. Landscape   t. Threatens

11. Gapped translation
a. La **contaminación** del aire se ha convertido en un **desafío** fundamental
b. La pérdida de la **biodiversidad** es un problema **universal**   c. El **deshielo** de los **polos** provoca inundaciones
d. El **calentamiento** global se **debe** a la contaminación
e. El efecto **invernadero** se **acelera** por la actividad humana   f. La **poblacion** mundial no **para** de aumentar
g. La temperatura de los **océanos** no **para** de crecer

12. Sentence puzzle
a. El efecto invernadero se acelera por la actividad humana
b. La población mundial no para de crecer
c. El deshielo de los polos amenaza la diversidad de la fauna
d. El desperdicio de los alimentos juega un papel importante en el agotamiento de los recursos naturales
e. El ser humano está dejando una huella cada vez mayor en el medio ambiente
f. La subida del nivel del mar contribuye a los desastres naturales en las zonas costeras
g. El sobreconsumo tiene una gran influencia en la escasez de alimentos

13. Tangled translation
a. La **población** mundial no deja de **crecer** cada **año**
b. El **deshielo** de los polos provoca **inundaciones**
c. La subida del **nivel** del **mar** contribuye a los **desastres** naturales
d. La **extinción** de especies animales **amenaza** la biodiversidad
e. El efecto **invernadero** se **acelera** por la actividad **humana**
f. El **agotamiento** de los **recursos** es un problema **universal**
g. El **calentamiento** global se debe a la **contaminación**
h. El **aumento** de la población **juega** un papel importante en la **escasez** de alimentos y los cambios en el **paisaje**

14. Translate into Spanish
a. El efecto invernadero   b. Calentamiento global   c. Escasez   d. Desperdicio de alimentos
e. Sobreconsumo   f. La especie humana   g. Paisaje   h. Cada año   i. El deshielo de los polos

15. Find the Spanish equivalent in the text
a. Hoy en día   b. En todo el mundo   c. Enfermedades respiratorias   d. Problemas de salud   e. Rápidamente
f. La extinción   g. En gran parte   h. Ahora sabemos   i. Causa   j. Mejorar   k. Condiciones de vida

16. Complete the translation
Another problem is the excessive usage of **resources**, which has a great **influence** on the exhaustion of natural
resources. We are **consuming** more than we can **afford**. Sources of non-renewable **fossils** such as carbon and **oil**
are running out and that is why we have to **look for** other sources of energy such as solar or wind energy.

17. Tick or cross
a. x b. x c. x d. x e. √ f. √ g. x h. √ i. x j. x k. √ l. x

18. Complete the sentences below based on the text
a. Serious natural disasters take **place** regularly   b. Air pollution generates **health problems**
c. The **human** species is making its **footprint** on the environment increasingly **visible**
d. Satisfy its **needs** and **improve** its life condition   e. Today we **consume** more than we can **afford**
f. We have to **look** for other sources of energy

19. Find in the text:
a. Natural   b. Grave   c. Regularmente   d. Desfortunadamente   e. Calentamiento   f. Generar   g. Agotamiento

20. Find the Spanish equivalent in the text
a. Agotamiento   b. Países   c. Futuro   d. Fertilizantes   e. Existir   f. Sin agua limpia   g. Del mismo modo
h. Ríos y lagos   i. Agricultura intensiva   j. Deslizamientos de tierra   k. Calentamiento global
l. Deshielo de los polos   m. Zonas costeras   n. Afecta

21. Answer the questions
a. Exhaustion of drinking water   b. Because life without clean water can't exist
c. Use of pesticides and chemical fertilizers   d. Intensive farming   e. Coastal towns are being lost
f. Erosion of coastal areas and decrease of living areas

22. Correct the following phrases
a. **El** peligro de **que** el agua potable se agote   b. El **nivel** del mar   c. Las zonas **costeras**
d. **Fertilizantes** químicos   e. Contaminación de **los manantiales**   f. Muchos países **en el** mundo

23. Translate into English the following phrases from paragraph 4
a. The sea advances   b. They are being lost   c. Are lost under water   d. Bit by bit
e. Living areas   f. This global phenomenon   g. At a social level

24. Complete with the options provided
Hoy en día, los **desastres** naturales ocurren **regularmente** en todo el **mundo**. La contaminación del **aire se ha** convertido en un gran **desafío** y genera **muchos** problemas de salud y enfermedades **respiratorias**. El **agotamiento** de los **recursos naturales** es otro problema **universal** que debemos solucionar **rápidamente** para salvar a nuestro planeta.

25. Split phrases
a. **El uso de pesticidas y fertilizantes químicos** lleva a la contaminación del suelo
b. Estamos consumiendo más **de lo que podemos permitirnos**
c. Este fenómeno global contribuye a **la disminución de las zonas habitables**
d. Ahora sabemos que el efecto invernadero **se acelera por la actividad humana**
e. El mar avanza **y se va perdiendo una calle a la vez**
f. La desaparición de especies animales **amenaza la diversidad de la fauna**
g. La especie humana está dejando **una huella visible en el paisaje**

26. Tiled translation
Hoy en día, hay cada vez más desastres naturales en todo el mundo. Es un fenómeno preocupante porque las tormentas se vuelven más fuertes y generan muchos daños a su paso. La temperatura global no para de aumentar y provoca el deshielo de los polos. Esto tiene impacto en el aumento del nivel del mar y provoca inundaciones y erosión en las zonas costeras en muchos países. El mar gana terreno constantemente a la tierra, lo que tiene como efecto la disminución de las zonas habitables a escala global.

27. Complete with the missing verb
a. La subida del nivel del mar **provoca** inundaciones en las zonas costeras
b. La población mundial no para de a**umentar** cada año
c. El sobreconsumo **juega** un papel importante en el agotamiento de los recursos naturales
d. El ser humano está d**ejando** una huella cada vez mayor en el paisaje
e. El deshielo de los polos **contribuye** a los desastres naturales, como por ejemplo las inundaciones
f. La desaparición de las especies animales **pone** en peligro la diversidad de la fauna
g. La contaminación del suelo se ha **convertido** en un problema universal
h. La pérdida de la biodiversidad **tiene** una gran influencia en el medio ambiente

28. Translate into Spanish
a. La población mundial no para de aumentar cada año
b. El sobreconsumo juega un papel importante en el agotamiento de los recursos naturales
c. La pérdida de la biodiversidad es un problema universal y pone en peligro la vida en la Tierra
d. El efecto invernadero se acelera por la contaminación y la actividad humana
e. El desperdicio de alimentos tiene una gran influencia en el medio ambiente
f. El aumento del nivel del mar causa inundaciones en las zonas costeras y es en parte responsable de los deslizamientos de tierra
g. El uso de los pesticidas y los fertilizantes químicos contamina el agua potable
h. De la misma manera, la agricultura intensiva genera la contaminación de ríos y lagos

29. Translate into Spanish
Hoy en día, la contaminación del aire se está convirtiendo en un desafío crucial para todos los países. Cada año

genera más y más enfermedades respiratorias y problemas de salud en todo el mundo.

Asimismo, la contaminación del agua es preocupante porque sin agua limpia no es posible la vida en la Tierra.

La agricultura intensiva es en parte responsable de la contaminación de ríos y lagos.

El uso de pesticidas y fertilizantes químicos para la agricultura también genera mucha contaminación en el campo.

En las zonas costeras, el mar gana terreno constantemente a la tierra, lo que tiene como efecto la disminución de las zonas habitables a escala global. Además, el aumento del nivel del mar provoca inundaciones en la costa.

30. Guided composition

Free writing

Unit 5. Environment: potential solutions

1. Match up
Los residuos – Waste   **Comprar** – To buy   **Se aconseja** – It is advised   **Prohibir** – To forbid
Reutilizar – To reuse   **Los árboles** – Trees   **Evitar** – To avoid   **La caza** – Hunting   **Frenar** – To slow down
Productos sostenibles – Sustainable products   **Es mejor** – It is better   **El agua de lluvia** – Rainwater
Proteger – To protect   **De un solo uso** – Single use

2. Choose the correct option
a. El comportamiento   b. Agua potable   c. Luchar   d. El aumento   e. Prohibir   f. Reutilizar   g. Regar
h. El desperdicio   i. Frenar   j. El uso   k. La colecta   l. Podemos   m. Es mejor

3. Sentence puzzle
a. Se aconseja   b. Reducir nuestro consumo de agua   c. Salvar nuestro planeta
d. Evitar sequías   e. Reducir el desperdicio de recursos   f. Comprar productos sostenibles
g. Reducir las actividades contaminantes   h. Reciclar la basura   i. Especies en peligro de extinción

4. Anagrams
a. Árboles   b. Basura   c. Sostenible   d. Prohibido   e. Residuos   f. Caza   g. Mejor   h. Proteger   i. Aumento

5. Gapped translation
a. To limit **overconsumption**   b. To collect **rainwater**   c. To buy **sustainable** products
d. To avoid **single** use products   e. To **slow down** deforestation   f. **Drinkable** water
g. We should ban **poaching**

6. Break the flow
a. Para conservar la Tierra   b. Para proteger a los animales   c. Se aconseja reciclar la basura
d. El comportamiento de la gente   e. Para salvar nuestro planeta   f. El desperdicio de recursos
g. La colecta de especies raras

7. Choose the correct translation
a. It is advised   g. To slow down   c. Droughts   d. The rise   e. It is better   f. Trees   g. The picking
h. Drinking water   i. To reduce   j. We should

8. Spot and supply the missing word
a. **Se** aconseja reciclar la basura   b. **Es** ético comprar productos sostenibles
c. Combatir la contaminación **del** suelo   d. Limitar el uso **de** agua potable
e. La caza de especies **en** peligro de extinción   f. Recoger agua **de** lluvia **para** regar
g. Cambiar el comportamiento **de** la gente   h. Para evitar la sequía hay **que** reducir el consumo
i. Es imprescindible prohibir **el** uso de los pesticidas

9. Match the words of similar meaning
Reducir – **Frenar**   Se aconseja – **Se recomienda**   Combatir – **Luchar**   Reciclar – **Reutilizar**
Esencial – **Imprescindible**   Dejar – **Parar**   Proteger – **Conservar**   Deberíamos – **Tenemos que**
Árboles – **Bosques**   Residuos – **Basura**

10. Sentence puzzle
a. Para evitar la sequía es necesario reducir nuestro consumo de agua
b. Para conservar la Tierra necesitamos cambiar el comportamiento de la gente
c. Para salvar nuestro planeta deberíamos limitar el uso del agua potable
d. Para proteger a los animales tenemos que prohibir la caza de especies en peligro de extinción
e. Para reducir el desperdicio de recursos es más ético comprar productos sostenibles

11. Wordsearch

R	E	D	U	C	I	R				S	O	S	T	E	N	I	B	L	E
E			S														A		S
G		C	O	M	P	O	R	T	A	M	I	E	N	T	O		S		E
A		A										V					U		N
R		Z						R	E	U	T	I	L	I	Z	A	R		C
		A	U	M	E	N	T	O				T					A		I
												A							A
											P	R	O	H	I	B	I	R	L

Hunting: **Caza** Behaviour: **Comportamiento** Rubbish: **Basura**
Sustainable: **Sostenible** To avoid: **Evitar** Essential: **Esencial**
Rise: **Aumento** To ban: **Prohibir** To reduce: **Reducir**
To reuse: **Reutilizar** Use: **Uso** To water: **Regar**

12. Spot the error and translate into English

a. Hay que prohibir la colecta de especies raras   b. **Para** frenar la deforestación podemos plantar **árboles**
c. **Es** vital limitar el uso del agua potable   d. Es **esencial** reducir las actividades contaminantes
e. Necesitamos evitar la sequía y salvar nuestro planeta
f. Se recomienda no comprar productos de un solo uso   g. Es mejor recoger el agua de **lluvia** para regar
h. Necesitamos conservar los bosques y no usar pesticidas   i. Es ético **reciclar** la basura

13. Translate into Spanish

a. Salvar nuestro planeta   b. Es necesario prohibir   c. Comprar productos sostenibles
d. Podemos plantar árboles   e. Tenemos que reciclar la basura   f. Cambiar el comportamiento de la gente
g. Proteger a los animales   h. La contaminación del suelo   i. Evitar los productos de un solo uso
j. Limitar el uso del agua potable

14. Definition game

a. Animales: Seres que viven, sienten y se mueven por su propia voluntad
b. Agua potable: Sustancia líquida que se puede beber sin riesgo de ponerse enfermo
c. Residuos: Materia inservible que resulta de la descomposición o destrucción de una cosa
d. Caza: Perseguir a un animal salvaje para matarlo
e. Sequía: Cuando no llueve durante un largo periodo de tiempo
f. Pesticidas: Productos químicos utilizados por agricultores para eliminar parásitos
g. Prohibir: Imponer que no se haga cierta cosa
h. Sobreconsumo: Comprar cosas de manera excesiva y sin necesidad
i. Deforestación: Cortar extensas superficies de bosques sin plantar árboles nuevos

15. Find the Spanish equivalent in the text

a. Para evitar problemas   b. El consumo de agua   c. Podemos cambiar
d. Utilizando el agua de lluvia para regar   e. Además   f. Del mismo modo, para reducir la basura
g. Evitar comprar   h. Regalar cosas que ya no usamos   i. A otras personas   j. Organizaciones benéficas
k. Venderlas en internet   l. Imprescindible

16. Faulty translation

To combat **air** pollution, it is essential to **reduce** polluting activities such as industrial emissions and air
transport which is using **oil** products, or the **industrial** emissions from factories. To fight against **soil** pollution,
it is essential to **reduce the use of** pesticides and **chemical** fertilisers and encourage **organic** farming.

17. Complete the sentences
a. Finally, to protect animals, we should **preserve their environment** and **slow down** deforestation
b. It's important to **plant trees** and to preserve **existing forests**
c. In addition, we should **ban** the hunting of **endangered** species and severely punish **poaching**

18. Complete with the missing vowels
a. **Organizaciones** benéficas   b. **La agricultura orgánica**   c. Los fertilizantes químicos   d. **La caza furtiva**
e. Productos derivados del petróleo   f. Plantar árboles

19. Translate into English
a. Finally   b. Environment   c. Their   d. Extinction   e. Punish   f. Existing

20. Find the Spanish equivalent in the text
a. **Comportamiento**   b. **Aprender**   c. **Menos**   d. **Para**   e. **Nuestra**   f. **Enseñar**   g. **Consumo**   h. **Propia**
i. **Fácil**   j. **Valioso**   k. **Todos podemos**   l. **La Tierra**   m. **Desarrollo**

21. Complete the translation
One of the big recent issues linked to **global warming** is that of the heat waves, which each year **cause**
devastating **fires.** When there is a **drought** the **ground/soil** is very dry, which favours the spread of **fire.** To stop
the rise in temperatures, it's important, among other things, to **plant trees** and to **preserve forests.**

22. Answer the following questions on paragraphs 3 & 4
a. Heat waves are closely linked to global warming and cause devastating fires every year
b. We should plant trees and preserve forests   c. To recycle waste
d. Having different bins helps in separating waste into recyclable and non-recyclable

23. Guided translation
a. **Para reducir el desperdicio de recursos**   b. **Para frenar el aumento de las temperaturas**
c. **Reducir nuestro consumo de agua**   d. **Necesitamos castigar severamente la caza furtiva**
e. **Es importante fomentar la conciencia**

24. Complete with the correct option choosing from the options below
Para combatir la **contaminación** del aire, es fundamental reducir las actividades contaminantes, como el
transporte que utiliza productos **derivados** del petróleo o las emisiones **industriales** de las fábricas. Para
combatir la contaminación del suelo, es **imprescindible** reducir el uso de los pesticidas y fertilizantes **químicos,**
al igual que fomentar la agricultura **orgánica** tanto como sea posible.
Finalmente, para proteger a los animales, primero **deberíamos** proteger el medio ambiente y frenar la
deforestación. Es importante **plantar** árboles y preservar los bosques **existentes.** Luego, deberíamos **prohibir** la
caza de especies en peligro de **extinción** y castigar severamente la caza **furtiva.**

25. Faulty translation
a. We **should** learn   b. The **exhaustion** of fossil resources   c. To **choose** local brands rather than big **companies**
d. The soil is very **dry** in times of drought   e. We **need to** limit the use of **drinking** water
f. It is **recommended** to recycle **rubbish**   g. It is necessary to **encourage ecological** farming
h. As **much** as possible   i. We can **give away** the stuff we don't use anymore
j. **Fortunately,** each problem **has** a solution

26. Translate into English
a. To fight against air pollution it's important to reduce polluting activities
b. To protect animals we have to ban the hunting of endangered species
c. To save our planet it is vital to change people's behaviour
d. To avoid droughts we need to collect rainwater for watering
e. It is essential to plant trees to slow down the deforestation and to recover forests
f. To reduce overconsumption one can donate items they no longer need to other people and organizations or sell
them second hand on the internet
g. Our consumption choices have a direct impact on the environment and it is better to buy sustainable products
h. There are many things we can do for our planet and the easiest thing is to start in your own home

27. Translate into Spanish

a. Deberíamos aprender a consumir menos   b. El actual ritmo mundial de consumo
c. Nuestras elecciones de consumo tienen un impacto directo en el medio ambiente
d. Las olas de calor causan los incendios cada año
e. Muchas de las grandes ciudades en el mundo tienen ahora un sistema de reciclaje
f. Es mejor comprar productos sostenibles de comercio justo
g. Necesitamos cambiar el comportamiento de la gente
h. Para evitar sequías, es vital limitar el uso de agua potable

28. Translate the following paragraphs into Spanish

Para luchar contra la contaminación del aire, es fundamental reducir las actividades contaminantes como los transportes que utilizan productos derivados del petróleo o las emisiones industriales de las fábricas. Para combatir la contaminación del suelo, es imprescindible prohibir los pesticidas y fertilizantes químicos y fomentar la agricultura orgánica tanto como sea posible.

Además, para frenar el agotamiento de los recursos, se aconseja reciclar la basura. Asimismo, para reducir los residuos se recomienda reutilizar objetos, o podemos regalar las cosas que ya no queremos a otra persona. ¡Reduce, reutiliza, recicla! Las tres cosas importantes que hacer para salvar nuestro planeta.

29. Complete with an appropriate word

a. Hay que fomentar la agricultura **orgánica**
b. Necesitamos limitar el **uso** del agua potable y **recoger** el agua de lluvia para regar
c. Es aconsejable **evitar** los productos de un **solo** uso
d. Para conservar **nuestro** planeta necesitamos cambiar el **comportamiento** de la gente
e. Para frenar la **deforestación** y conservar los **bosques** es imprescindible **plantar** árboles
f. Para proteger a los **animales** debemos prohibir la **caza** de especies raras

30. Write a 140-word text

Free writing

Unit 6. What I study, what I like/dislike and why

1. Match up
El arte – Art   **Estoy aprendiendo** – I am learning   **Asignatura** – School subject   **Entretenido** – Entertaining
Bachillerato – Sixth form   **Lo que odio** – What I hate   **Sin embargo** – However   **Útil** – Useful
Complicado – Complicated   **Estoy estudiando** – I am studying   **Química** – Chemistry   **Difícil** – Difficult
Clase – Lesson   **Aburrido** – Boring

2. Sentence puzzle
a. Estoy estudiando arte   b. Estoy aprendiendo química   c. Porque es muy interesante
d. Porque es complicado   e. Porque es demasiado difícil   f. Porque es muy útil
g. Porque pienso que es   h. Porque me parece interesante   i. Lo que odio   j. Mi clase favorita
k. Me encanta esta asignatura   l. Porque es muy aburrido

3. Complete the words and translate them into English
a. Cre**ativo**: Creative   b. Co**legio**: School   c. Las mat**emáticas**: Maths   d. Est**oy** est**udiando**: I am studying
e. Bast**ante** fácil: Quite easy   f. Compli**cado**: Complicated   g. Bac**hillerato**: Sixth form   h. Diver**tido**: Fun
i. Ú**til**: Useful   j. **Las ciencias**: Science

4. Faulty translation
a. I am studying **art**   b. It's **very** easy   c. I **prefer** this subject   d. It's **useful**   e. It's very **boring**
f. In **the sixth form**   g. I **love**   h. I love **IT**   i. It's **too** complicated

5. Translate into English
a. I am learning physics   b. I am studying history   c. I am interested in geography   d. I like this subject
e. What I can't stand is homework   f. This year I am studying Spanish   g. What I don't like at all is physics
h. IT is too complicated

6. Positive or negative
a. Positive   b. Negative   c. Positive   d. Positive   e. Negative   f. Negative   g. Positive   h. Negative   i. Positive

7. Wordsearch

E				H					Q					D					
L		A	S	I	G	N	A	T	U	R	A			I					
F				S					Í					F	Á	C	I	L	
U	V			T					M					Í			I		
T	I	N	F	O	R	M	Á	T	I	C	A			C		T		E	
U	D			R					C					I	Ú		T		
R	A			I				B	A	C	H	I	L	L	E	R	A	T	O
O				A	B	U	R	R	I	D	O				A				

Subject: **Asignatura**   Art: **Arte**   History: **Historia**
Difficult: **Difícil**   Useful: **Útil**   Easy: **Fácil**
Sixth form: **Ba**chillerato   IT: **Informática**   The future: El **futuro**
Chemistry: **Q**u**í**mica   Boring: **Aburrido**   Life: **V**ida

8. Broken sentences
a. Esta asignatura es **bastante fácil y útil**   b. Actualmente **estoy aprendiendo física**
c. Lo que **detesto es la historia**   d. Prefiero **estudiar inglés**   e. Me parece que **el dibujo es creativo**
f. Estoy estudiando **en la universidad**   g. Me interesa la **informática**   h. Para mí el arte **es muy entretenido**

 THE LANGUAGE GYM

9. Gapped translation
a. Estoy estudiando **química**   b. Estoy **aprendiendo** historia   c. Me interesa el **arte**   d. Mi clase **favorita**
e. Lo que **odio**   f. Porque es **demasiado** difícil   g. Porque es **aburrido**   h. Esta **asignatura**   i. **Realmente** útil

10. Complete with the correct verb
a. Lo que **prefiero** estudiar es la educación física   b. Por ahora estoy **estudiando** arte en el colegio
c. Me **interesan** las ciencias y las matemáticas   d. Lo que prefiero **estudiar** en el instituto es arte
e. **Estoy** aprendiendo matemáticas   f. Odio los deberes porque **me llevan** mucho tiempo

11. Translate into Spanish
a. Instituto   b. Estudiar   c. Entretenido   d. Bachillerato   e. Deberes   f. Historia   g. Informática   h. Fácil
i. Difícil

12. Slalom writing
a. Me encanta esta asignatura   b. Lo que odio son los deberes   c. Porque me parece emocionante y útil
d. Porque es demasiado complicado   e. Mi clase favorita es arte   f. Pienso que es muy enriquecedor
g. En mi opinión es bastante fácil

13. Guided translation
a. Lo que **más** me **gusta** estudiar   b. Lo que no me gusta nada   c. **Porque** me lleva mucho **tiempo**
d. **Porque** es **demasiado difícil**   e. En mi **opinión** es relajante   f. Lo que no **soporto** es la **informática**
g. **Por ahora** me **interesa la química**   h. Este año estoy aprendiendo historia
i. De m**o**mento estoy estudiando teatro   j. Me **encanta** esta **asignatura**

14. Complete with an appropriate word (accept other correct answers)
a. Desde hace un año **estoy** estudiando teatro
b. Lo que prefiero estudiar son las matemáticas **porque** son realmente útiles
c. Mi **asignatura** favorita es educación física porque es muy **divertida/emocionante/motivadora**
d. Me **gusta/encanta** esta asignatura porque me parece muy enriquecedora y **muy/bastante** fácil
e. Por el **contrario,** lo que odio es la historia porque me **aburre** profundamente
f. Sin **duda/embargo,** mi clase favorita es la de **física/arte/etc.** porque **pienso/creo** que es bastante interesante
g. Me interesa esta disciplina porque en mi **opinión** es emocionante y **motivadora/entretenida/etc.**
h. **Este** año **estoy** estudiando inglés en el bachillerato

15. Sentence puzzle
a. Este año estoy aprendiendo teatro e historia en el colegio
b. Actualmente estoy estudiando química y física en el bachillerato
c. Lo que más me gusta estudiar es el inglés porque es muy entretenido
d. Lo que prefiero estudiar es arte porque en mi opinión es relajante
e. Mi clase favorita es la de educación física porque me parece emocionante y motivadora
f. Por el contrario, no me gustan los deberes porque me llevan mucho tiempo

16. Split sentences
a. Por ahora estoy estudiando **química en el instituto**: At the moment I am studying chemistry in high school
b. Lo que prefiero estudiar **es arte e inglés**: What I prefer to study is art and English
c. No me gustan nada los **deberes porque son aburridos**: I don't like at all homework because it is boring
d. No soporto la física porque **en mi opinión es muy difícil**: I can't stand physics because in my opinion it is difficult
e. Mis asignaturas favoritas son **historia y geografía**: My favourite subjects are history and geography
f. Lo que odio sobre **todo son las ciencias**: What I hate above all is science
g. En mi opinión el arte es **muy enriquecedor**: In my opinion art is very enriching

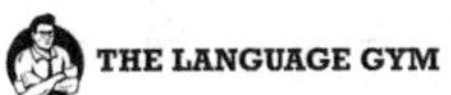

17. Translate into Spanish

a. Lo que más me gusta estudiar es el arte porque es muy creativo

b. Me encanta esta asignatura porque creo que es bastante interesante

c. En mi opinión es bastante fácil

d. Lo que odio son los deberes porque me llevan mucho tiempo

e. Me gusta la geografía porque me parece emocionante y útil

f. No me gustan las ciencias porque me parecen demasiado complicadas

g. Me interesa la física porque pienso que es muy enriquecedora

h. Este año estoy aprendiendo historia y química

i. Lo que no me gusta nada es la informática porque es demasiado difícil

18. Find the Spanish equivalent in the text

a. Estoy estudiando   b. Me encanta esta asignatura   c. Realmente útil para el futuro   d. Me gustaría estudiar
e. Además   f. Más adelante   g. Muy útil para viajar   h. Trabajar en el extranjero   i. Me gustaría ser actor

19. Complete the translation of paragraph 3

On the **other** hand, I hate **math** because it is too difficult and I find it **boring**. Moreover, **what** I don't like is homework because it takes a **lot of** time and I prefer to do something **more** interesting. Unfortunately, I have no other **option** and I have to do it, otherwise my **teachers** and parents tell me off.

20. Find in paragraph 4 the following words

a. Demasiado: **Too much**   a. Historia: **History**   c. Aburrimiento: **Boredom**   d. Complicada: **Complicated**
e. Vida: **Life**   f. Ordenadores: **Computers**

21. Circle the correct verb

a. Aprendiendo   b. Encanta   c. Estoy estudiando   d. Me parece   e. Me aburre   f. Ser   g. No soporto

22. Translate into English

a. Finalmente   b. Por el contrario   c. Actualmente   d. En el extranjero   e. En mi opinión   f. Emocionante
g. También

23. Find the Spanish equivalent in the text

a. Desde hace un año   b. Me gustaría ser   c. Voy a estudiar   d. En el futuro   e. Por ahora
f. Me parece muy difícil   g. Me parece que   h. Tampoco   i. A veces   j. Son demasiado difíciles
k. No es muy útil   l. Sé que

24. True, false or not mentioned

a. False   b. False   c. True   d. Not mentioned   e. False   f. True   g. True   h. False   i. Not mentioned   j. True

25. Answer the following questions about the text

a. She would like to be an engineer   b. She finds it difficult   c. Gratifying and easy
d. She likes art because it's relaxing and creative at the same time
e. She can't stand biology because it bores her to death   f. She thinks it is not very useful

26. Guided translation

a. Me gustaría estudiar en la universidad b. Es muy conveniente para viajar   c. También me gusta el teatro
d. Por eso es importante para mí   e. Me parece bastante interesante   f. Paso más de dos horas
g. Me aburro profundamente en las clases   h. Al mismo tiempo   i. No tengo otra opción
j. Me gustaría trabajar en el extranjero

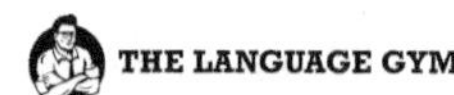

27. Translate into Spanish

a. Mi clase favorita es la de física porque pienso que es muy enriquecedora e interesante

b. Me encanta esta asignatura porque pienso que es bastante fácil y realmente útil

c. Sin embargo, lo que odio son las matemáticas porque son demasiado difíciles

d. No me gustan nada los deberes porque me llevan mucho tiempo y son aburridos

e. Me gusta el arte porque me parece relajante y entretenido

f. No me gusta química porque es demasiado complicada para mí

g. Estoy interesado/a en el teatro porque me parece motivador y creativo al mismo tiempo

h. De momento estoy aprendiendo historia y geografía en el bachillerato

i. Finalmente lo que no soporto es la informática porque odio los ordenadores

28. Translate into Spanish

Me llamo Violeta y soy de Málaga, en el sur de España. Tengo 16 años y vivo con mis padres y mis dos hermanas. Tenemos una casa en el campo, no muy lejos de la ciudad.

En este momento estoy estudiando química y física en el bachillerato. También estoy aprendiendo geografía y me parece interesante y bastante fácil.

Mi asignatura favorita es física porque pienso que es emocionante. Además, también me gusta el arte porque es relajante y creativo.

Sin embargo, lo que no me gusta nada es la historia, ya que me aburro profundamente durante las clases.

En el futuro me gustaría estudiar física en la universidad porque es importante para ser ingeniera. También me gustaría estudiar matemáticas ya que es muy útil en la vida.

29. Guided composition

Free writing

Unit 7. My post 16 plans

1. Choose the correct translation
a. This week   b. I want   c. I think that   d. Decision   e. I will take   f. Abroad   g. To carry on studying
h. I am going to choose   i. I will take my time   j. I am going to study

2. Match up
En el extranjero – Abroad   **Tomarme mi tiempo** – To take my time
Una decisión difícil – A difficult decision   **Creo que** – I believe that   **Quiero** – I want
Para mis A levels – For my A Levels   **Voy a estudiar** – I am going to study   **Probablemente** – Most likely
Compromiso – A commitement   **Prácticas** – Work experience   **Voy a elegir** – I am going to choose
Estudios superiores – Further studies   **Todavía no sé** – I don't know yet   **Esta semana** – This week

3. Complete with the correct word
a. Me gustaría hacer unas **prácticas** laborales   b. Este trabajo me **interesa** porque es variado
c. Voy a tomarme mi **tiempo**   d. Voy a elegir una **carrera** de derecho   e. Es un compromiso a **largo** plazo
f. **De** momento, creo que voy a trabajar de albañil   g. No tengo ni **idea** de lo que voy a estudiar
h. Ojalá pueda **seguir** estudiando y hacer A Levels

4. Translate into English
a. I am going to study Spanish   b. I am going to choose maths   c. I would like to go abroad
d. I prefer to reflect calmly   e. I think I will stop studying   f. If I could I would take a gap year
g. I am passionate about it because it is enriching

5. Break the flow
a. Es una decisión importante   b. Creo que voy a elegir   c. Tengo la intención de
d. Todavía no sé lo que quiero hacer   e. De momento voy a trabajar   f. Voy a seguir estudiando
g. En la industria hotelera

6. Wordsearch

B	A	C	H	I	L	L	E	R	A	T	O								R	E
	E	L	E	G	I	R						P	R	Á	C	T	I	C	A	S
		C	A	R	R	E	R	A							M				J	T
									E	N	T	O	N	C	E	S			E	U
	S	A	M	O	I	D	I								J				D	D
															O					I
F	O	N	T	A	N	E	R	O			C	O	M	P	R	O	M	I	S	O
					P	E	L	U	Q	U	E	R	A							S

Plumber: **Fontanero**   Better: **Mejor**   Work experience: **Prácticas**
To choose: **Elegir**   Languages: **Idiomas**   Commitment: **Compromiso**
Studies: **Estudios**   To quit: **Dejar**   Hairdresser: **Peluquera**
Career: **Carrera**   Baccalaureate: **Bachillerato**   So: **Entonces**

7. Missing letters
a. Voy a elegir   b. Dejaré de estudiar física   c. Voy a trabajar como albañil
d. Creo que me tomaré un año sabático   e. Si pudiera me gustaría seguir estudiando
f. No tengo ni idea de lo que voy a hacer   g. Tengo la intención de estudiar medicina
h. Ojalá pueda hacer A Levels   i. Este trabajo me interesa   j. Porque está bien pagado

THE LANGUAGE GYM

8. Complete

a. El próximo año me gustaría **hacer** A Levels   b. De **momento** voy a buscar trabajo como camarero
c. Creo que voy a **dejar** de estudiar economía   d. Si pudiera, haría prácticas **laborales**
e. Me **tomaré** un año sabático en el extranjero   f. Es un compromiso a **largo** plazo
g. Después de mis exámenes voy a trabajar **en** ventas   h. Prefiero tomarme mi tiempo y **reflexionar** con calma
i. Voy a **elegir/estudiar** humanidades   j. Cuando **haya** terminado el instituto seguiré estudiando

9. Spot and supply

a. Me apasiona este trabajo porque es variado y además está muy **bien** pagado
b. Si pudiera, me gustaría tomarme un año **sabático** en el extranjero. Quiero viajar a América Latina
c. El próximo año, **después** de mis exámenes voy a hacer prácticas laborales
d. Me gustaría hacer un grado de ciencias y trabajar en la universidad **como** astrofísico
e. Es una **decisión** importante, así que quiero tomarme mi tiempo y reflexionar con calma
f. Para mis estudios superiores **quiero** hacer un grado de idiomas
g. Tengo la intención de **obtener/hacer/estudiar** un grado en comercio
h. De momento voy a **buscar** trabajo en la industria hotelera

10. Sentence puzzle

a. El próximo año me gustaría hacer el bachillerato
b. Si fuera posible, haría unas prácticas laborales de peluquero
c. Si pudiera, me tomaría un año sabático en Argentina
d. Después, en la universidad, me gustaría estudiar química
e. Es una decisión importante, así que prefiero tomarme mi tiempo
f. Todavía no sé lo que quiero hacer, pero probablemente una carrera médica

11. Tangled translation

a. No **tengo** ni idea de lo **que** voy a **estudiar**
b. Dejar el teatro o las **matemáticas** es **una** decisión **difícil**
c. Si **pudiera** me tomaría un **año sabático** en el **extranjero**
d. Este **trabajo** me apasiona **porque es** variado y **está** bien **pagado**
e. El **próximo** año me gustaría **mucho** hacer el **bachillerato**
f. **Después**, en la universidad, voy a **elegir** humanidades **e** idiomas
g. **Si** fuera posible, haría unas **prácticas laborales** de **albañil**
h. Ojalá **pueda** encontrar **trabajo cuando** haya **terminado** el instituto
i. Es un **compromiso** a largo **plazo**, así que es **mejor** reflexionar con **calma**

12. Translate into Spanish

a. Si pudiera   b. Voy a elegir   c. Me gustaría estudiar   d. Hacer A Levels   e. Voy a hacer   f. Es difícil
g. El extranjero   h. Para hacerme   i. Por eso prefiero

13. Guided translation

a. Si **pudiera**, me **tomaría** un **año sabático**
b. Si **fuera** posible, haría unas **prácticas laborales** de **fontanero**
c. No es fácil elegir, **entonces** prefiero **tomarme** mi **tiempo**
d. **Cuando haya** terminado el **instituto**, me **gustaría** hacer A Levels.
e. El **próximo** año voy a **estudiar** español y **química**
f. Este **trabajo** me **interesa porque** es agradable y está bien **pagado**

14. Find the Spanish equivalent in the text

a. Cuando termine   b. En el extranjero   c. Voy a seguir estudiando   d. Saco buenas notas   e. Para mejorar
f. Es posible que   g. Todavía no sé   h. Un año sabático   i. Montar mi propio negocio
j. La protección del medio ambiente   k. Tomarme mi tiempo   l. Ir a la universidad

15. Complete the translation

I **still** don't know what I'm going to do **next** year, but I'm probably going to **choose** humanities because I love foreign **languages** and I'm not **good** at science. For now, **during** the holidays, I'm going to **look** for a job as a **waitress**.

16. Answer the following questions in English
a. To be with her friends and to prepare well for the university   b. Foreign languages
c. Cristina will probably choose a degree in business   d. She is not good at science
e. To set up her own business related to the protection of the environment or recycling
f. She would like to go to England or Canada so she can improve her English

17. True, false or not mentioned
a. True   b. False   c. True   d. Not mentioned   e. True   f. False   g. True

18. Translate into Spanish
a. Hacer el bachillerato   b. Todavía no sé   c. Voy a hacer   d. Compromiso a largo plazo
e. Es mejor tomarme mi tiempo   f. Estudiar en el extranjero   g. Montar mi propio negocio

19. Find the Spanish equivalent in the text
a. Algo relacionado   b. Probablemente   c. Fontanero   d. Un pueblo pequeño   e. Me parece   f. Estoy buscando
g. Prácticas laborales   h. Disponible

20. Complete with the help of the text
a. **Hay** más opciones   b. Pedir **consejo** a un asesor   c. La **industria** hotelera   d. Quizás **haya** alguna manera
e. Combinar **ambos** campos   f. No es **fácil** elegir   g. **Podría** ser muy útil   h. **Tomarme** mi tiempo
i. **Además,** están bien pagados   j. Una vez que **termine**   k. No tengo **ni** idea   l. Estoy **buscando** información

21. Answer the following questions in English
a. Santiago lives in a small town
b. He would like to carry on his studies in a city
c. Santiago is interested in the hospitality industry, engineering and administration
d. He would like to work in the construction industry as a plumber or an electrician
e. He wants to move to a city because there are more options to find work experience and later on a good job
f. He would choose engineering or administration for his further education

22. True, false or not mentioned
a. True   b. Not mentioned   c. True   d. Not mentioned   e. True   f. False   g. False

23. Match up
Si me animo – If I decide   **Relacionado** – Related   **Consejo** – Advice   **Ambos** – Both   **Desafío** – A challenge
Está mejor pagado – It´s better paid   **Bachillerato** – Baccalaureate   **Asesor** – Advisor

24. Complete the Spanish sentences
a. **Hacer** el bachillerato   b. Tener buenas **notas**   c. Los idiomas **extranjeros**   d. Voy a **elegir**
e. **Montar** mi propio negocio   f. Las ciencias no se me **dan** bien   g. Quiero **prepararme** bien
h. Vale la **pena** intentarlo   i. La industria **hotelera**   j. **Está** mejor pagado

25. Complete using the options provided below
Es una **decisión** difícil porque me gusta mucho tanto el español como la historia. Es un compromiso a **largo**
plazo, así que es mejor **tomarme** mi tiempo y pensar con **calma**.
En la **universidad** quiero hacer un grado de **empresariales**. Además me gustaría mucho estudiar en el
extranjero para mejorar mi inglés. Por eso es posible que me **tome** un año **sabático** y vaya a **Inglaterra** o a
Canadá.

26. Translate into Spanish
a. Cuando termine mis estudios   b. Me gustaría hacer A Levels   c. Voy a elegir idiomas extranjeros
d. Es difícil elegir   e. Quiero tomarme mi tiempo   f. Me gustaría montar mi propio negocio
g. Es posible que vaya   h. Es un trabajo interesante   i. Si saco buenas notas
j. Me gustaría trabajar en el extranjero   k. Voy a pasar un año en Argentina   l. Quiero hacer una carrera médica

27. Spot and supply the missing word
a. Merece la **pena** intentarlo   b. Me gustaría **seguir** estudiando para prepararme
c. **Es** una decisión importante y difícil   d. Me gustaría trabajar **en** el extranjero
e. De momento **voy** a buscar trabajo en ventas   f. Si pudiera **haría** una carrera como actriz
g. No tengo ni idea de lo **que** voy a estudiar   h. Voy a **tomarme** un año sabático e iré a México
i. Creo que voy a **elegir** humanidades   j. Este trabajo me apasiona **porque** es gratificante
k. El próximo año voy a dejar de **estudiar** historia   l. Haría unas **prácticas** laborales de fontanero

28. Complete with an appropriate word
a. Si fuera posible **seguiría** estudiando para prepararme mejor **para** ir a la universidad
b. El próximo año voy a **buscar** trabajo en la industria hotelera
c. Todavía no **sé** muy bien lo que quiero hacer, pero **probablemente** una carrera científica
d. Creo que voy a **dejar** de estudiar matemáticas y me centraré **en** el teatro
e. Pienso que **merece** la pena intentarlo porque **podría** ser muy útil en el futuro
f. Para mí es difícil **elegir** una carrera porque…
g. …me interesan **tanto** los idiomas extranjeros como **la** medicina
h. Cuando haya **terminado** el instituto voy **a** tomarme un año sabático y viajaré **por** Europa
i. Me gusta este **trabajo** porque es interesante y además **está** muy bien pagado
j. Para mis estudios **superiores** estoy contemplando **hacer/estudiar/obtener** un grado en comercio

29. Translate into Spanish
a. Si pudiera me tomaría un año sabático
b. Si fuera posible, haría unas prácticas laborales de albañil
c. El próximo año voy a estudiar inglés y voy a dejar el arte
d. Si pudiera, me gustaría montar mi propio negocio
e. Voy a pasar un año en Zaragoza para mejorar mi español
f. Prefiero trabajar como médico porque me parece gratificante
g. Después de mis exámenes, voy a buscar trabajo como camarero
h. Es una decisión importante, entonces prefiero tomarme mi tiempo
i. Esto me apasiona porque es agradable y variado
j. Para mis estudios superiores, estoy contemplando hacer una carrera literaria

30. Translate the following paragraphs into Spanish
El próximo año me gustaría hacer A Levels en mi pueblo para estar con mis amigos. Me gustaría estudiar química porque me parece muy interesante.
Creo que voy a elegir ciencias y voy a dejar el inglés y el arte porque los dos me parecen demasiado difíciles. Después, si puedo, me tomaré un año sabático en el extranjero. Me gustaría pasar un año en España para perfeccionar mi español. Voy a buscar trabajo de camarera o en la industria hotelera o en ventas para poder hablar español todos los días.
En la universidad me gustaría hacer un grado en química. Después, si fuera posible, me gustaría trabajar como ingeniera para una empresa farmacéutica.

31. Guided composition
Free writing

Unit 8. What job I would like to do and why

1. Match up
Estudiar medicina en la uni – To study medicine at university   **Viajar** – To travel
Ayudar a los demás – To help others   **La carrera de mis sueños** – My dream career   **Quiero** – I want
Hacer una carrera – To make a career   **Podría** – I could   **Prefiero** – I prefer
Ser contable – To be an accountant   **Trabajar como artesano** – To work as a craftsman
Hacerme cirujano/a – To become a surgeon

2. Spot and correct the 6 wrong translations
a. √   b. √   c. Accountant   d. Office   e. They say   f. √   g. Today   h. √   i. I could   j. To be   k. √

3. Sentence puzzle
a. Cuando termine mis estudios, me gustaría trabajar como cirujano
b. A mi parecer es una actividad que está en auge en este momento
c. Mis padres me dicen que debería hacer carrera en ventas
d. En cuanto a mí, prefiero trabajos de oficina
e. Según mis amigos debería trabajar como entrenador
f. Es la carrera de mis sueños porque me parece variada y bien pagada

4. Complete the table
According to my parents – **Según mis padres**   Office jobs – **Trabajos de oficina**   I could – **Podría**
I should work – **Debería trabajar**   It seems – **Parece**   Varied and well paid – **Variado/a y bien pagado/a**
To help others – **Ayudar a los demás**   I want to become – **Quiero hacerme**

5. Complete with the correct option
a. **Considero** que   b. **Hacerme** cirujano   c. **Hacer** carrera   d. En **ventas**   e. Trabajar **como** artesano
f. Bastante **lucrativo**   g. Mis padres me **dicen**   h. Es la carrera de mis **sueños**

6. Translate into English
a. I would like to become a lawyer   b. As soon as I graduate   c. Outdoor jobs   d. According to my friends
e. It is a trendy sector   f. Because it seems tiring   g. I want to do this job   h. But it doesn't seem well paid
i. It will allow me to work in a team   j. Once I have my diploma in the bag   k. In sales

7. Definition game
a. Llegar   b. Peluquero/a   c. Trabajo   d. Estresante   e. Oficina   f. A mi parecer   g. Hacerme / Hacerse
h. Debería   i. Viajar   j. Cirujano

8. Wordsearch: find the Spanish translation of the words below

A	G	R	I	C	U	L	T	O	R			E	S	T	U	D	I	O	S
				A								X							E
	A	P	A	R	E	C	E		A	C	T	I	V	I	D	A	D		G
	C			R				S				G							Ú
	T			E				U	N	I	V	E	R	S	I	D	A	D	N
	R			R				E				N							
V	I	A	J	A	R			Ñ				T	R	A	B	A	J	O	
	Z							O				E							

Job: **Trabajo**
According to: **Según**
Studies: **Estudios**
University: **Universidad**

Farmer: **Agricultor**
Demanding: **Exigente**
Career: **Carrera**
To travel: **Viajar**

It Seems: **Parece**
A dream: **Sueño**
Actress: **Actriz**
Activity: **Actividad**

9. Complete with the missing vowels
a. **En auge** b. **Ingeniero** c. **Llegar a ser** d. **Carrera** e. **Independiente** f. **Artesano** g. **Al aire libre**

10. Split phrases
a. Prefiero los trabajos **al aire libre** b. Me gustaría trabajar **como artesana**
c. Ser agricultor me **parece gratificante** d. Mi abuelo me dice **que debería ser médico**
e. Una vez tenga mi título **quiero trabajar en una oficina** f. Es la carrera de mis **sueños, aunque es muy difícil**
g. En mi opinión, ser cirujano **es muy estresante** h. Debería estudiar **medicina en la universidad**

11. Gapped English-to-Spanish translation
a. Cuando **termine** mis estudios b. En **cuanto** a mí c. Me gustaría **hacerme** d. Quiero **trabajar**
e. Parece **exigente** f. Es la **carrera** de **mis** sueños g. Me gustaría **llegar** a ser h. Parece **gratificante**
i. Trabajos al aire **libre** j. Trabajos de **oficina**

12. Spot and supply the missing words
a. **En** mi opinión, es una industria bastante lucrativa b. Me gustaría llegar **a** ser peluquero
c. Es la carrera **de** mis sueños d. Mis padres me dicen que debería estudiar medicina **para** hacerme cirujano
e. **En** cuanto me gradúe voy a trabajar f. Creo que es un sector **en** auge
g. Por lo tanto podría trabajar **como** artesano h. Prefiero trabajos **al** aire libre
i. Eso me permitirá ayudar a **los** demás

13. Complete with the missing letters
a. Trabajar como entrenador b. En cuanto me gradúe c. Cuando termine mis estudios
d. Hacerme ingeniero mecácnico e. Es la carrera de mis sueños f. Una industria bastante lucrativa
g. Quiero hacer este trabajo h. Mi hermano me dice

14. Anagrams
a. Trabajar como artesano b. Gratificante, pero no muy bien pagado c. Está de moda en este momento
d. Trabajo independiente e. Una vez tenga mi título f. Hacer una carrera en ventas
g. La carrera de mis sueños h. En cuanto a mí

15. Complete with an appropriate word
a. Mi hermano me dice que **debería** estudiar medicina
b. Me gusta esta profesión porque me **permitirá** ayudar a los demás
c. Según mis amigos, es un sector que está en **auge**
d. Un **trabajo** independiente es exigente
e. Cuando **termine** mis estudios quiero trabajar como pescador y vivir en un pueblo en la costa
f. Me **parece** que ser contable es un trabajo aburrido
g. Una vez tenga mi **título** en el bolsillo me gustaría trabajar como artesano
h. Quiero hacer este trabajo porque creo que es gratificante, aunque no muy bien **pagado**
i. Hacer carrera en **ventas** me parece agotador
j. Prefiero trabajar en equipo al aire **libre** o como entrenador deportivo
k. Me gustaría trabajar en el **extranjero**

16. Guided translation
a. **En cuanto a mí**   b. **Los trabajos al aire libre**   c. **Considero**   d. **En mi opinión**   e. **Una vez tenga mi título**
f. **Quiero trabajar**   g. **Los trabajos de oficina**   h. **Me gustaría hacerme**   i. **Me gustaría trabajar**
j. **Como artesano**   k. **Como cirujano**   l. **Mis padres dicen que**   m. **Parece que**

17. Find the Spanish equivalent in paragraph 1
a. Es bastante agotador   b. Un gran problema   c. Este trabajo   d. Parece   e. Puedes cambiar   f. Me fascina
g. Me gustaría ayudar   h. Espero   i. Las personas   j. Mantenerse sanas

18. Complete the translation
My brother **tells** me that I could do a **gap year** in Costa Rica and work as a diving **instructor**. I must **admit** that
I am **passionate** about this activity, but maybe not **to the point** of making it my job. Also, if I were a **doctor** I
could afford to go on **vacation** to Costa Rica. It is one of the most beautiful countries in the world and you can
see sloths in **the wild**!

19. Spot and supply the missing words
Personalmente **preferiría** trabajar en un hospital y **ayudar** a los demás, por lo que el trabajo de médico **sería**
perfecto. Además, **me** gusta el trabajo **en** equipo y en un hospital **nunca** se trabaja solo. El **sector** médico
también es uno de los **más** importantes, ya que **su** objetivo es **cuidar** a las personas y salvar **vidas**.

20. Tick and cross

a. X   b. √   c. √   d. X   e. √   f. X   g. X   h. √   i. √   j. X

21. Translate into English
a. It would be perfect   b. To work in a hospital   c. To save lives   d. Its objective   e. Is to look after people
f. You never work alone

22. True, false or not mentioned
a. True   b. True   c. False   d. True   e. False   f. False   g. False   h. Not mentioned   i. False

23. Find the Spanish equivalent in the text
a. Es la carrera de mis sueños   b. Bien pagada   c. Estoy estudiando   d. Debería intentar   e. Odio   f. Dicen que
g. Estudiar medicina   h. Por otro lado   i. Tener éxito   j. Una buena manera   k. Al aire libre   l. En la oficina
m. Debo desarrollar

24. Faulty translation
Finally, to **be** a good architect, it is necessary to be creative, demanding and accurate. These are qualities that I
must develop if I want to **be successful** in this sector. It is **also** important to have some knowledge of the history
of art and it is essential to master the **software** of technical design. In my **opinion**, it is an activity which is **fast-
growing**, **therefore**, there is a **strong** competition in the architecture sector.

25. Word hunt
a. **Profesión**   b. **En mi opinión**   c. **Variado**   d. **En auge**   e. **Realmente**   f. **Al aire libre**   g. **Dominar**
h. **Preciso**

26. Complete with the missing words

a. En cuanto me **gradúe**, me gustaría trabajar en ventas   b. Quiero h**acerme** piloto de avión

c. Porque me **permitirá** viajar   d. Mis amigos me dicen que **debería** trabajar como entrenador de fútbol

e. Mis padres creen que debería hacer una **carrera** como abogado   f. Prefiero trabajar al **aire** libre

g. No me gustan n**ada** los trabajos de oficina

h. Es la carrera de mis **sueños** porque es creativa, variada y bastante bien **pagada**

27. Guided English-to-Spanish translation

a. **Trabajos de oficina**   b. **Trabajos al aire libre**   c. Me **gustaría hacerme**   d. Mis **padres dicen**

e. **Cuando termine mis estudios**   f. **Esto me permitirá**   g. **Quiero trabajar como**

h. Es la **carrera de mis sueños**   i. **En cuanto a mí**   j. **Me gusta este trabajo**   k. **Parece exigente**

28. Translate into Spanish

a. Estudios   b. Cirujano   c. Contable   d. Preciso   e. Trabajo   f. Gratificante   g. Quiero

h. Hacerme/Llegar a ser   i. Ingeniero   j. Prefiero   k. Al aire libre   l. Oficina   m. En mi opinión

n. Para mí   o. Me gusta   p. Carrera   q. Mi propia empresa   r. Como entrenador   s. Quiero trabajar

t. Me gustaría ser

29. Spot and supply the missing word

a. Trabajar **como** artesano   b. Carrera **en** ventas   c. **Me** permitirá viajar   d. Está **en** auge

e. Que **es** bastante lucrativo   f. Estudiar **en** la universidad   g. Pero no está muy bien **pagado**

h. Una **vez** tenga mi título en el bolsillo   i. Me encanta trabajar **en** equipo

30. Translate into Spanish

a. Despues de mis estudios me gustaría llegar a ser contable

b. En mi opinión en una industria en auge

c. Me gustaría tener mi propia empresa en la industria del software

d. En mi opinión es un trabajo muy lucrativo

e. Prefiero los trabajos que están bien pagados y son variados

f. Mis padres dicen que debería trabajar como profesor

g. Según mi hermano, debería ser instuctor de buceo o entrenador deportivo

h. No quiero trabajar como abogado porque pienso que es aburrido

i. Este trabajo me permitirá ayudar a los demás y trabajar en equipo

j. Me gusta esta profesión porque quiero un trabajo autónomo

Unit 9. Home, town, neighbourhood and region

1. Match up

En la planta baja – On the ground floor   **Un edificio** – A building   **Está limpio** – It's clean
En las afueras – On the outskirts   **Es demasiado ruidoso** – It´s too noisy   **Una habitación** – A room
En mi calle – In my street   **Mi barrio** – My neighbourhood   **Tiendas** – Shops   **Hay** – There is/are
Cosas que ver – Things to see   **Estación de autobuses** – A bus station   **Está muy sucio** – It´s very dirty
En casa – At home

2. Spot and correct the 6 wrong translations

a. A flat   b. A house   c. √   d. √   e. √   f. In the countryside   g. A dining room   h. √   i. It's dangerous
j. √   k. √   l. There are beaches   m. √

3. Sentence puzzle

a. Vivo en una casa en el campo   b. Vivo en un piso en las afueras   c. En el primer piso hay cinco habitaciones
d. En casa hay una cocina, un salón, un comedor y tres habitaciones
e. En mi pueblo hay una estación de tren, tiendas, un centro comercial y un supermercado
f. En mi región hay muchas actividades para los turistas

4. Complete the table

A train station – **Una estación de tren**   On the outskirts – **En las afueras**   We have – **Tenemos**
At home – **En casa**   An airport – **Un aeropuerto**   It's too noisy – **Es demasiado ruidoso**
Historical places – **Lugares históricos**

5. Complete with the correct option

a. En la **planta** baja   b. Pero no hay **tiendas**   c. Hay **seis** habitaciones   d. Está **limpio** y es tranquilo
e. En mi **calle**   f. No **hay** un estadio

6. Translate into English

a. I live in   b. In the mountain   c. In my town   d. A library   e. A bathroom   f. At the bus station
g. Amusement parks   h. A swimming pool   i. Good restaurants   j. On the outskirts   k. Historical places

7. Definition game

a. **Parque**   b. Las a**fueras**   c. **Biblioteca**   d. **Barrio**   e. **Campo**   f. **Sucio**   g. **Centro comercial**   h. **Bar**
i. **Tranquilo**   j. **Contaminado**   k. **Playa**

8. Wordsearch

B	I	B	L	I	O	T	E	C	A									T	
		A								A		P	L	A	Y	A		I	
T	U	R	I	S	T	A	S			F	L	I	M	P	I	O		E	
	C	R								U		S						N	
	A	I		S	U	P	E	R	M	E	R	C	A	D	O			D	
	M	O								R		I						A	
	P	L	A	N	T	A	B	A	J	A		N	R	U	I	D	O	S	O
	O									S		A							

Supermarket: **Supermercado**   Library: **Biblioteca**   Beach: **Playa**
Neighbourhood: **Barrio**   Tourists: **Turistas**   Noisy: **Ruidoso**
Outskirts: **Afueras**   Swimming pool: **Piscina**   Clean: **Limpio**
Ground floor: **Planta baja**   Countryside: **Campo**   Shops: **Tiendas**

9. Complete with the missing vowels
a. **Edificio** b. **Afueras** c. **Cafetería** d. **Estación de autobuses** e. **Espacios** verdes f. **En la primera planta**
g. **Cosas que ver** h. **Cuarto de baño**

10. Split sentences
a. No me gusta mi **ciudad porque está sucia** b. En mi calle hay **un bar y una panadería**
c. Vivo en un **chalet en la montaña** d. En mi región **hay lugares históricos**
e. Desafortunadamente no **tenemos una piscina** f. En mi casa hay una cocina, **un salón y dos habitaciones**
g. Me gusta mi barrio **porque está limpio** h. Tenemos parques de **atracciones y una cafetería**

11. Gapped translation
a. En mi **calle** b. Es **bonito** y está **limpio** c. Vivo en un **piso/apartamento**
d. En **casa** e. **Hay** ocho **habitaciones** f. Mi **barrio…** g. …es **ruidoso** h. Me **encanta** mi **pueblo**
i. Hay una **estación** de **autobuses** j. Una **casa** en la **costa** k. **Está** demasiado **contaminado**

12. Spot and supply the missing words
a. Un cuarto **de** baño b. Vivo **en** un edificio moderno c. **En** mi calle tenemos **una** cafetería
d. Odio **mi** pueblo porque **es** demasiado tranquilo e. En mi región hay muchos **espacios** verdes
f. En **el** segundo piso tenemos tres **habitaciones** g. Vivo **en** un chalet en **el** centro
h. **Hay/tenemos** una biblioteca, tiendas y restaurantes i. En **casa** hay una cocina, un salón y un dormitorio
j. Desafortunadamente no **hay** zonas peatonales k. **Me** encanta mi barrio porque es tranquilo

13. Complete with the missing letters
a. Actividades **para** los turistas b. En la montaña c. Es ruidoso y sucio
d. En mi calle hay un centro comercial e. Vivo en un piso en las afueras f. En mi región no hay playas
g. Un edificio en el centro de la ciudad h. Cosas que hacer para los jóvenes

14. Sentence puzzle
a. Desafortunadamente no tenemos un aeropuerto b. En casa tenemos dos cuartos de baño y una cocina
c. En mi pueblo hay una estación de tren y un supermercado
d. Pero no hay restaurantes buenos ni una biblioteca e. Me gusta mi ciudad porque es bonita y está limpia
f. Vivo en una casa en las afueras de una ciudad grande
g. En mi región hay muchas actividades para los turistas
h. Vivo en el segundo piso de un edificio moderno en el centro

15. Complete with an appropriate word (accept other correct answers)
a. Vivo en un **piso** en la **playa**
b. En la **primera/segunda** planta hay un **comedor/cuarto de baño** y una cocina
c. En mi ciudad **hay** muchas **cafeterías/tiendas/bibliotecas**
d. Tenemos **parques** de atracciones y playas
e. Mi **barrio** es feo y peligroso
f. No hay **zonas** peatonales
g. Odio mi pueblo **porque** está muy contaminado
h. **Vivo** en una casa en **el** campo
i. Hay un centro **comercial** con muchas **tiendas**
j. Me **gusta** mi barrio porque tenemos una **piscina/tienda/cafetería**
k. En mi piso hay cinco **habitaciones** y un **salón/comedor/cuarto de baño**
l. Mi **piso/apartamento** está en la **planta** baja

16. Guided translation
a. **Desafortunadamente** b. Mi **pueblo está limpio** c. Es **muy ruidoso** d. Un **piso** e. Un **supermercado**
f. **Tenemos una cocina** g. **Parques de atracciones** h. **En la primera planta** i. **Espacios verdes**
j. **Una zona peatonal** k. **Dos cuartos de baño** l. **Muchas tiendas**

17. Find the Spanish equivalent in the text
a. Las afueras b. Bastante c. Planta d. En casa e. En la ciudad f. Ordenada g. Bonito h. Tenemos
i. Cuarto de baño j. En la planta baja

18. Complete the translation
My city is called Bilbao and it is **located** in the north of Spain in the Basque Country region. I **love** it because it is very **pretty**, modern and always **clean**. My favorite part of the city is the Nervión **river**. Along the **river bank** there is a **pedestrian** area with parks, bars and restaurants, but the most **famous** site is the ultra-modern Guggenheim **museum**.

19. Translate into English
a. Hiking   b. Traditional dishes   c. Historical places   d. A lot of people speak   e. An official language
f. Does not resemble Spanish at all   g. The interesting thing is

20. Tick and cross
a. X b. X c. √ d. X e. √ f. √ g. X h. X i. √ j. X

21. Spot and supply the missing words (from paragraph 5)
En mi región hay muchas **actividades** para los turistas. Se **puede** practicar senderismo, visitar las playas o **los** pequeños pueblos típicos del País Vasco y por supuesto degustar **platos** vascos típicos como el marmitako, un guiso de **atún**. Donde vivo hay muchos espacios **verdes** y está lleno de lugares históricos. Lo **interesante** es que aquí mucha gente **habla** euskera. Es el otro idioma **oficial** del País Vasco y no se **parece** para nada al español. Gero arte! ¡Hasta **luego**!

22. True, false or not mentioned
a. True b. False c. True d. True e. Not mentioned f. True g. False h. False i. False j. True
k. Not mentioned

23. Find the Spanish equivalent in the text
a. Junto al mar   b. Se encuentra   c. Sur   d. Puedo hacer   e. Cuando quiera   f. En la planta baja   g. Una oficina
h. Un ático   i. Para guardar cosas   j. Una panadería   k. Rodeada   l. Mucho encanto

24. Faulty translation
You **can** get to Cádiz with practically any means of transport, be it car, train or **boat**. The train is an **excellent** option. The train station is located in the city centre, just **outside** the old town walls. Cádiz has a very special **location** – it is on a **small** peninsula, so it is totally **surrounded** by the sea. Also, it is an **old** fishing **town** so it has a lot of charm and tourists **can** visit various **historical** places. I **love** living here!

25. Word hunt
a. **Cocina** b. **Sur** c. **Estación** d. **Ático** e. **Panadería**   f. **Kayak, vela** g. **Pesquera**

26. Complete with the missing words
a. Vivo en las a**fueras** de una ciudad   b. En mi casa h**ay** tres habitaciones
c. Mi barrio está **sucio** y es **peligroso**   d. Tenemos un **cuarto** de baño
e. Me gusta mi **barrio** porque es tranquilo   f. En mi pueblo hay muchas zonas **verdes**
g. En mi ciudad hay dos **parques**   h. Cerca hay un centro comercial y un b**ar**
i. En la **planta** baja hay un salón   j. Aquí vienen muchos **turistas**   k. Puedes visitar varios **lugares** históricos

27. Guided translation
a. Mi casa es muy **luminosa**   b. Se **puede hacer senderismo**   c. Es demasiado **ruidoso**
d. **Puedo** hacer **deporte** e. En mi **barrio**   f. El **dormitorio** de mi hermano   g. **Junto** al **mar**
h. **Tiene** m**ucho** encanto   i. No se **parece** nada   j. En la **orilla** del río   k. Tenemos una oficina

28. Translate into Spanish

a. Me gusta mi barrio, pero a veces es demasiado ruidoso durante el fin de semana

b. En casa tenemos ocho habitaciones y hay dos plantas

c. Me encanta mi región porque hay muchas cosas que hacer para los jóvenes

d. En verano puedes ir a la playa y nadar en el mar. ¡Es genial!

e. En mi calle hay muchas tiendas y cafeterías. Siempre hay mucha gente

f. Me gusta vivir en la montaña porque puedo hacer senderismo

g. Me encanta vivir cerca del mar porque puedo hacer deportes acuáticos cuando quiera

h. En la planta baja tenemos una cocina, un salón y un comedor

i. No me gusta mi pueblo porque está sucio, es peligroso y está contaminado

j. En mi región hay muchas actividades para los turistas

29. Translate the following paragraphs into Spanish

Me llamo Carmen y vivo en Salamanca, en el este de España. Vivo en una casa grande en las afueras con mi familia. En casa, en la planta baja hay una cocina, un salón, un comedor, el dormitorio de mis padres y un baño. En la primera planta hay cinco habitaciones: el dormitorio de mi hermana, mi dormitorio, un baño, una sala de juegos y una oficina. Mi habitación favorita es mi dormitorio porque es luminosa, está ordenada y es espaciosa. Me gusta mi pueblo porque es bonito y limpio y hay muchas cosas que hacer para los jóvenes. Desafortunadamente, en verano hay muchos turistas y a veces es demasiado ruidoso porque hay mucho tráfico.

30. Guided composition

Free writing

Unit 10. Travel and tourism

1. Match up
El año pasado – Last year   **Pasé** – I spent   **Iré** – I will go   **Me alojé en** – I stayed in   **En avión** – By plane
Alquilé una bici – I rented a bike   **A Italia** – To Italy   **Este verano** – This summer   **Fui** – I went
Será divertido – It will be fun   **Saldré** – I will go out   **Durante las vacaciones** – During the holidays
Dos semanas – Two weeks   **Fue** – It was

2. Spot and correct the 6 wrong translations
a. √   b. √   c. By plane   d. I rented a car   e. √   f. In the morning   g. √   h. √   i. I will travel by train   j. √
k. √   l. Next year   m. I will spend one month

3. Sentence puzzle
a. Fui de vacaciones a Alemania con mi familia   b. Me gustaría ir de vacaciones a Suiza porque es muy bonita
c. El año que viene iré a Italia a ver a mis abuelos   d. Me alojé en un albergue juvenil
e. Pasé dos semanas en España. ¡Fue genial!   f. Viajé en coche y luego alquilé una bici

4. Complete the table
Fui – **Iré**   Alquilé – **Alquilaré**   Pasé – **Pasaré**   Viajé – **Viajaré**   Hice – **Haré**   Tomé – **Tomaré**
Me alojé – **Me alojaré**

5. Complete with the correct option
a. Un albergue **juvenil**   b. El año **pasado**   c. **Viajaré** a Inglaterra   d. Será **divertido**
e. Tomé el sol en la **playa**   f. Viajaré en **autobús**

6. Translate into English
a. I will travel by train   b. It was interesting   c. In the afternoon   d. I will rent a motorhome/caravan
e. Next year   f. I will spend a week   g. I travelled by train   h. I will go to the north of Europe   i. It will be great
j. I went out to the cinema   k. This year I went to Greece

7. Definition game
a. **Barco**   b. **Avión**   c. **Semana**   d. **Vacaciones**   e. **Aburrido**   f. **Lago**   g. **Museo**   h. **Mes**   i. **Italia**   j. **Tarde**
k. **Albergue**

8. Wordsearch

J							I	N	T	E	R	E	S	A	N	T	E		
U					V														
V	A	C	A	C	I	O	N	E	S			L	A	G	O				S
E		O			A	B	U	R	R	I	D	O		R					E
N		S			J									E					M
I		T			A									C	O	C	H	E	A
L		A	D	U	R	A	N	T	E					I					N
					É					I	N	G	L	A	T	E	R	R	A

Holidays: **Vacaciones**   During: **Durante**   Car: **Coche**
Interesting: **Interesante**   Week: **Semana**   Youth: **Juvenil**
England: **Inglaterra**   Coast: **Costa**   Lake: **Lago**
I will travel: **Viajaré**   Greece: **Grecia**   Boring: **Aburrido**

THE LANGUAGE GYM

9. Complete with the missing vowels
a. Relajante   b. Tomar el sol   c. Alquilaré   d. Me alojaré   e. Viajaré   f. Una semana   g. Visitas guiadas
h. En barco

10. Split phrases
a. El año pasado fui de **vacaciones con mi familia**   b. Pasaré dos semanas en **Francia. ¡Será genial!**
c. Por la mañana iré al museo **y luego visitaré a mis amigos**   d. Por la noche fui **a un restaurante**
e. Este verano me **gustaría ir a Alemania**   f. Viajaré en avión y luego **alquilaré una autocaravana**
g. Por la tarde tomé el sol **en la playa**   h. Durante las vacaciones **me alojaré en un hotel**

11. Gapped translation
a. **Viajé** en avión   b. Este **verano** iré a España   c. Me **alojé** en un hotel   d. Alquilé un **coche**
e. Visité unos **museos**   f. **Pasé** un mes allí   g. Fue muy **relajante**   h. **Será** genial   i. Iré a **Inglaterra**
j. **Viajaré** en barco   k. El año que **viene**

12. Spot and supply the missing words
a. Tomé **el** sol en **el** lago   b. Fui a Italia con mi familia. ¡Fue **genial!**   c. Alquilaré **una** bicicleta e iré **a** la playa
d. Pasaré un **mes** en la montaña   e. Viajaré en tren, **será** cómodo   f. **Por** la noche fui a un restaurante a cenar
g. **Me** alojaré en un albergue juvenil   h. Me gustaría **ir** de vacaciones con mis amigos
i. Visitaré muchos **monumentos** históricos   j. Pasé dos **semanas/meses** en la casa de mis abuelos
k. Durante las **vacaciones** haré turismo todos los días

13. Complete with the missing letters
a. Me alojaré en un hotel en el centro   b. **H**ice turismo en Francia y fu**e** interesante
c. Viajaré **c**uatro horas en avión   d. Pas**é** tres días en un camping   e. Será aburrido
f. Por la noche saldr**é** a la discoteca   g. M**e** gustaría viajar a Inglaterra
h. Alquilaré una autocaravana e iré al lago

14. Anagrams: sentences
a. Este año iré a Suiza   b. Por la mañana me gustaría hacer turismo   c. Tomaré el sol en la playa
d. Pasaré tres días en un albergue en la montaña   e. Me alojaré en una casa en el campo
f. El año pasado hice turismo en Alemania   g. Visitaré a mis abuelos en Francia   h. Por la noche iré a un bar

15. Complete with an appropriate word (accept any other correct answers)
a. Visité monumentos **históricos**   b. Por la mañana **haré/hice** turismo
c. **Pasaré/pasé** una semana en la casa de mis tíos   d. Viajaré en tren y **luego** alquilaré un coche
e. Después de comer, iré a la **playa** a tomar el sol   f. El año pasado **fui/viajé** a Inglaterra. ¡Fue genial!
g. Me gustaría hacer **visitas** guiadas   h. Por la noche **salí/saldré** a la discoteca
i. Me alojé en un albergue **juvenil** en la **montaña**   j. El **próximo** año viajaré a Grecia con mi familia
k. **Durante** las vacaciones me quedaré en casa   l. Será relajante, **pero** un poco aburrido

16. Guided translation
a. **Cinco días**   b. **En la playa**   c. **Dos semanas**   d. **Por la tarde**   e. **Un albergue juvenil**   f. **Iré a España**
g. **Viajaré**   h. **Pasaré un mes**   i. **Hice un poco de turismo**   j. **En la montaña**   k. **Alquilé una bici**
l. Me **gustaría** ir

17. Find the Spanish equivalent in the text
a. Alemania   b. Pasamos   c. Dos semanas   d. Allí   e. Nos alojamos   f. De tres estrellas   g. Primera   h. Luego
i. Un camping   j. Segunda

18. Complete the translation
It was my first **time** in Germany and I **loved** it because there were many activities for **young** people and there
was also a lot to **see**. We traveled by car for **almost** seven hours. It was quite exhausting, but **very** comfortable.

19. Spot and supply
Durante la **primera** semana estuvimos en Colonia. Es una ciudad grande **con** muchos monumentos históricos.
Visitamos la catedral **y** algunos museos y caminamos por el casco **antiguo**. También hicimos una ruta guiada **en**
bicicleta a lo largo **del** río Rin y me encantó porque **fue** original e hicimos deporte al **aire** libre al mismo tiempo.

20. Tick and cross
a. √ b. X c. √ d. X e. √ f. X g. X h. √ i. √ j. X

21. Translate into English the words and phrases below taken from paragraph 4
a. Afterwards b. Close to the lake c. A trip d. I was reading e. I enjoyed f. Every morning
g. A lot of green spaces

22. True, false or not mentioned
a. True b. Not mentioned c. False d. True e. True f. False g. False h. False i. True j. Not mentioned
k. False

23. Find the Spanish equivalent in the text
a. Por primera vez b. Había c. Me encantó d. Visita guiada e. Mi vuelo f. Ir a nadar g. Tomé
h. Un equilibrio ideal i. Famosos j. El mismo país k. Hasta las tres de la mañana l. Inolvidables

24. Faulty translation
I went out for **dinner** every night **with** my **boyfriend. After** dinner we went out to bars and then to clubs until
three in the **morning.** They were **unforgettable** holidays and **next year** I would **love** to return to Spain. **Next**
time I would like to **visit** Madrid.

25. Word hunt
a. Me **encantó** b. **Gigantesco** c. **Vuelo** d. **Inolvidable** e. **Nadar** f. **Famoso** g. **Sitio**

26. Complete with the missing words
a. Lo q**ue** me encanta b. **Pasaré** dos semanas en casa de mis tíos c. Ir de **vacaciones**
d. **Tomé** el sol en la playa e. Mi vuelo duró tres h**oras** y media f. Viajaré en **barco** a Italia
g. El año pasado **fui** a Inglaterra h. Fueron unas vacaciones **inolvidables** i. Hice una **v**isita guiada
j. Había muchas **actividades** al aire libre k. Será **cómodo,** pero agotador

27. Guided translation
a. **Pasamos** b. **Nos alojamos** c. **Había** d. **Fue** b**astante agotador** e. **Visitamos** f. **Nunca** vi g. **Ir a n**a**dar**
h. **Tomé el sol** i. **Mi sitio favorito** j. **F**uimos en b**arco** k. **Una excursión a la montaña**

28. Translate into Spanish
a. El año pasado fui de vacaciones a Alemania. ¡Fue genial!
b. Viajé en avión y luego alquilé un coche
c. El viaje duró tres horas y fue bastante agotador, pero cómodo
d. Me alojé en un hotel en el centro de la ciudad durante una semana
e. Hice una visita guiada de los monumentos más famosos. Fue interesante
f. Por la noche salí al restaurante con mi familia
g. También visité muchos museos, pero en mi opinión fue un poco aburrido
h. El año que viene iré a Barcelona y viajaré al este del país
i. Pasaré dos semanas en la playa
j. Fueron unas vacaciones inolvidables. Me gustaría volver a Inglaterra el verano que viene

29. Translate the following paragraphs into Spanish
El año pasado fui de vacaciones a Francia por primera vez. Viajé en avión y el vuelo fue bastante agotador, pero
muy cómodo. El viaje duró cuatro horas.
Me alojé en un albergue juvenil en Lyon y la gente era muy acogedora. El primer día hice una visita guiada en
autobús. Mi lugar favorito fue el casco antiguo, porque era muy bonito y estaba limpio.
El segundo día alquilé una bicicleta y fui al lago. Tomé el sol y nadé. ¡Fue genial! Por la noche comí en un
restaurante y luego salí con unos amigos.
El año que viene me gustaría volver a Francia, pero en invierno. Me gustaría ir a esquiar porque parece divertido
y también un poco arriesgado.

30. Guided composition
Free writing

Unit 11. Sport

1. Match up
Ciclismo – Cycling **Haré** – I will do **Gané** – I won **Emocionante** – Thrilling **Escalada** - Rock climbing
Motivador – Motivating **Perdí** – I lost **Después del colegio** – After school **A veces** – Sometimes
Cuando puedo – When I can **Los deportes de equipo** – Team sports **Vela** – Sailing
Submarinismo – Scuba diving **Hago** – I do

2. Spot and correct the 6 wrong translations
a. When I can b. √ c. It's more competitive d. √ e. √ f. √ g. Last week h. I won i. √ j. √
k. I never play l. √ m. Horse riding n. √

3. Sentence puzzle
a. Juego al fútbol una vez a la semana b. Prefiero los deportes de equipo porque son más divertidos
c. A veces nado d. Nunca juego al golf e. Ayer hice vela f. Mañana haré ciclismo

4. Complete the table
In the swimming pool – **En la piscina** I don't play – **No juego** I train – **Entreno** Rock climbing – **Escalada**
I swim – **Nado** I lost - **Perdí** Team sports – **Deportes de equipo**

5. Complete with the correct option
a. Cada **sábado** b. Hago **ciclismo** c. Me gustaría **probar** d. Es demasiado **agotador** e. Hice **senderismo**
f. Cuando **puedo**

6. Translate into English
a. I never play b. It's too tiring c. From time to time d. I sailed e. It was very challenging
f. Three times a week g. My favourtie sport h. I train one hour every week i. It's very difficult
j. When I have time k. If I could, I would do yoga

7. Definition game
a. **Submarinismo** b. **Ping pong** c. **Escalada** d. **Natación** e. **Mañana** f. **Demasiado** g. **Baloncesto**
h. **Equipo** i. **Esquí** j. **Senderismo** k. **Individual**

8. Wordsearch

						P							E					A	
	C	U	L	T	U	R	I	S	M	O	P	I	N	G	P	O	N	G	
	U					E							T		I			O	
N	A	D	A	R		F							R		S			T	
	N		M	O	T	I	V	A	D	O	R		E	S	C	A	L	A	R
	D					E							N		I			D	
	O	D	I	V	E	R	T	I	D	O			O		N			O	
	E	Q	U	I	P	O									A			R	

Bodybuilding: **Culturismo** Table tennis: **Ping pong** When: **Cuando**
I prefer: **Prefiero** Tiring: **Agotador** Fun: **Divertido**
To swim: **Nadar** Team: **Equipo** To rock climb: **Escalar**
Motivating: **Motivador** Swimming pool: **Piscina** I train: **Entreno**

9. Complete with the missing vowels
a. Divertido b. Vela c. Normalmente d. **Atletismo** e. **Jugaré** f. **Submarinismo** g. **Gané** h. **Si pudiera**

10. Split phrases
a. Después del **colegio juego al bádminton**   b. Hago atletismo tres **veces a la semana**
c. Ayer hice senderismo y **estuvo genial**   d. Nunca juego al golf **porque es demasiado difícil**
e. Cuando puedo, hago **ciclismo y natación**   f. Mi deporte favorito **es el baloncesto**
g. Me gustaría **probar el parapente**   h. Lo hago porque, aunque es **agotador, es divertido**

11. Gapped translation
a. **Hice** vela   b. A veces **juego** al fútbol   c. Entreno a **menudo**   d. Haré **senderismo**   e. Fui al **polideportivo**
f. No **juego** al tenis   g. Me encanta jugar al **voleibol**   h. Quiero **probar** hacer yoga   i. **Entreno** cuando puedo
j. Todos los **fines** de semana   k. Mi **deporte** favorito

12. Spot and supply the missing words
a. Después **del** colegio juego al ping pong.   b. Entreno una hora **al** día en el gimnasio
c. Ayer **jugué** al rugby, pero perdí   d. Nunca **hago** submarinismo
e. Mi deporte favorito **es** la escalada   f. Prefiero hacer **deportes** de equipo
g. Me gusta el atletismo **porque** es competitivo   h. A veces entreno **en** el polideportivo
i. **Si** pudiera, me gustaría probar el esquí   j. Cuando **puedo** hago natación
k. Me gusta porque **es** desafiante y emocionante

13. Complete with the missing letters
a. **Porque** es motivador y competitivo   b. Me encanta el **culturismo**   c. Me gustaría probar el submarinismo
d. No me gustan los deportes de equipo   e. Todos los fines de semana   f. Ayer hice senderismo
g. Mañana jugaré al bádminton   h. El tenis es demasiado difícil

14. Anagrams: sentences
a. Por las tardes tengo entrenamiento de boxeo con mi prima
b. Cuando tengo tiempo hago natación en la piscina de mi casa
c. Mi deporte favorito es la escalada porque es desafiante   d. Por lo general me gusta hacer deportes de equipo
e. Ayer jugué al tenis y le gané a mi hermano   f. Nunca hago culturismo porque me parece demasiado agotador
g. Si pudiera me gustaría probar el patinaje sobre hielo   h. Cuatro veces a la semana hago gimnasia artística

15. Complete with an appropriate word
a. Cuando **puedo**, hago boxeo con mi amigo   b. Ayer **jugué** al tenis y fue muy divertido
c. De **vez** en cuando voy al gimnasio y hago yoga   d. Me gustaría **probar** el esquí
e. Nunca juego al golf porque me **parece** aburrido   f. Normalmente juego al fútbol **todos** los días
g. Mañana **jugaré** al bádminton con mi hermana   h. Cada viernes voy a la montaña y hago **senderismo**
i. No me gustan los **deportes** individuales   j. Si **pudiera**, me gustaría probar el submarinismo
k. Mi deporte **favorito** es la equitación   l. **Me gustan** los deportes de equipo porque son divertidos

16. Guided translation
a. **Todos los sábados**   b. **En el gimnasio**   c. **Una vez a la semana**   d. **Es demasiado agotador**
e. **Por lo general**   f. **Me gustaría probar**   g. **Haré**   h. **Parece** divertido   i. **Es bastante competitivo**
j. **Es emocionante**   k. **En la piscina**   l. **Con mi primo/a**

17. Find the Spanish equivalent in the text
a. Deportista   b. Entreno   c. Cinco veces   d. Mi deporte favorito   e. Juego   f. Mi equipo local   g. Desde
h. También formo parte de   i. El año pasado

18. Complete the translation
Every **Monday**, I do **athletics** at the **stadium** with my **colleagues**. On **Tuesdays**, I do **strength training** at the **gym**. On Wednesdays, I **rest** at home and I do my **homework**, I **read** or I **study** my favourite **subjects**. On Thursdays, I **train** with my **team** at the **sports centre** near my house. Finally, on Fridays, I go **swimming** at the local **swimming pool** with my **brother** and my **sister**.

19. Spot and supply the ten missing words
Todos **los** sábados tengo un partido. A veces jugamos **en** casa y eso **me** encanta porque tenemos a todos nuestros seguidores en el estadio y es motivador. Por **el** contrario, cuando jugamos fuera, a veces tenemos que **ir** muy lejos. Entonces **es** agotador porque tenemos que **pasar** muchas horas en el autobús. Ayer **fue** genial porque le ganamos a **uno** de los mejores equipos de **nuestra** región.

20. Translate into English the following words from paragraph 2
a. I have a match   b. Sometimes   c. At home   d. Outside   e. Far away   f. We won   g. To spend many hours

21. Tick and cross
a. X   b. √   c. X   d. √   e. √   f. X   g. √   h. X   i. √   j. X

22. True, false or not mentioned
a. True   b. False   c. True   d. Not mentioned   e. True   f. False   g. False   h. True   i. False   j. Not mentioned
k. False

23. Find the Spanish equivalent in the text
a. Deportes acuáticos   b. Un lugar   c. Viento   d. En verano   e. Participan   f. Pertenezco al club   g. Iré
h. Carrera   i. Encontrar   j. Si pudiera   k. Bastante arriesgado   l. Al mismo tiempo

24. Spot and correct the 10 errors in the translation of paragraph 4
If I could, I would like to **try** martial arts because I am fascinated by **combat** sports and Bruce Lee's films.
On the other hand, I **never** play **racquet** sports because I am **bad** and I find them **boring**. One day I would also
like to do **rock climbing** in the **mountains** as it's quite **risky** and **challenging** at the same time.

25. Word hunt
a. **Navegar**   b. **Puerto**   c. **Regata**   d. **Patrocinadores**   e. **Mi sueño es**   f. **Malo**   g. **Mientras tanto**
h. **Escalar**

26. Complete with the missing words
a. Me g**usta** el voleibol   b. Iré en b**icicleta** con mi padre
c. Es un **lugar** ideal para hacer vela   d. Mi d**eporte** favorito es el baloncesto   e. Ga**né** un campeonato
f. **Todos** los lunes hago atletismo   g. Pertenezco al **club** de mi pueblo   h. Formo **parte** del equipo regional
i. Los d**eportes** de raqueta me aburren   j. Intentaría patinar sobre **hielo**   k. Mientras tanto tengo que **entrenar**

27. Guided translation
a. **Soy d**eportista   b. **Desde que tenía cinco años**   c. **Casi todos los fines de semana**   d. **Hago culturismo**
e. **Las artes marciales**   f. **Me parece aburrido**   g. **Es mi sueño**   h. **El próximo fin de semana**
i. **Fue genial**   j. **Me gustaría probar**

28. Translate into Spanish
a. El fin de semana pasado gané una carrera. ¡Fue genial!   b. Si pudiera, me gustaría probar las artes marciales
c. Me gusta escalar, pero es bastante arriesgado   d. Nunca juego al golf, es demasiado difícil
e. El próximo fin de semana iré al puerto   f. Mañana jugaré al bádminton con mi hermano
g. Mi deporte favorito es la equitación   h. Ayer jugué al fútbol con mis amigos
i. Se me da mal el tenis, pero me encanta jugar al ping pong   j. Me gustaría hacer yoga tres veces a la semana

29. Translate the following paragraphs into Spanish
Una vez a la semana juego al vóleibol con mis amigos. Me gusta porque es divertido y relajante. Después del
colegio, a veces también hago atletismo con mi hermano. Me parece bastante difícil.
Cuando tengo tiempo, hago ciclismo con mi padre. Generalmente vamos bastante lejos. Es agotador pero
divertido al mismo tiempo. Prefiero los deportes individuales porque son más competitivos.
El fin de semana pasado jugué al ping pong en el polideportivo, pero desafortunadamente perdí la competición.
También hice senderismo con mi familia y fue genial.
El próximo fin de semana haré culturismo y el domingo jugaré al bádminton con mi hermana. Después iré de
compras al centro comercial con mi novia.

30. Guided composition
Free writing

Unit 12. Customs and festivals

1. Match up
Regalos – Gifts   **A la iglesia** – To church   **Febrero** – February   **Los musulmanes** –Muslims
Compartir – To share   **Celebramos** – We celebrate   **El Día de la Madre** – Mother's Day
Parientes – Relatives   **La Navidad** – Christmas   **La mezquita** – The mosque   **En casa** – At home
Año Nuevo – New Year   **Los cristianos** – Christians   **Nos juntamos** – We meet up

2. Spot and correct the 7 wrong translations
a. Every year   b. √   c. Father's Day   d. Easter   e. √   f. The Three Kings   g. √   h. Fireworks   i. √   j. √
k. A temple   l. To pray to god   m. √

3. Sentence puzzle
a. En mi casa celebramos el Año Nuevo   b. Los cristianos van a la iglesia
c. En mi familia celebramos el Día de los Muertos   d. Hay fuegos artificiales y desfiles
e. Mis padres me dan regalos   f. Los judíos van a la sinagoga

4. Complete the table
Holidays – **Vacaciones**   To share – **Compartir**   Processions – **Desfiles**   Gifts – **Regalos**   Mosque – **Mezquita**
They get together – **Se reúnen**   Mother's Day – **El Día de la Madre**

5. Complete with the correct option
a. Rezan a su **dios**   b. Durante esta **fiesta**   c. **Veo** a mi familia   d. Recibo **regalos**   e. Los días **festivos**
f. **Compartir** una comida festiva

6. Translate into English
a. It's my favourite festival   b. I see my friends   c. We celebrate the Day of the Three Kings
d. The Christians pray in the church   e. The Muslims go to the mosque   f. The Jews meet up in the synagogue
g. I love fireworks   h. The Hindus go to the temple   i. The families share a festive meal   j. To have a good time
k. I'm on holiday

7. Definition game
a. **Dios**   b. **Regalos**   c. **Año Nuevo**   d. **Mercadillo**   e. **Enero**   f. **Mezquita**   g. **Navidad**   h. **Pascua**
i. **Día de la Madre**   j. **Sinagoga**   k. **Religioso**

8. Wordsearch

				C	R	I	S	T	I	A	N	O	S						
		D			E			D		C	O	M	P	A	R	T	I	R	
		E			Z	F		I	T	E	M	P	L	O			G		
P	A	S	C	U	A	I		O									L		
		F			R	E		S	M	U	S	U	L	M	A	N	E	S	
		I				S	P	A	R	I	E	N	T	E	S	I	S		
		L				T											I		
F	U	E	G	O	S	A	R	T	I	F	I	C	I	A	L	E	S	A	

Muslims: **Musulmanes**   Fireworks: **Fuegos artificiales**   Temple: **Templo**
Church: **Iglesia**   To pray: **Rezar**   God: **Dios**
To share: **Compartir**   Festival: **Fiesta**   Easter: **Pascua**
Christians: **Cristianos**   Relatives: **Parientes**   Procession: **Desfile**

9. Complete with the missing vowels
a. Celebramos   b. **El Año Nuevo** c. Cada año   d. Recibo   e. Musulmanes   f. Rezar a Dios   g. Desfiles
h. Fuegos artificiales

10. Split phrases
a. En México celebramos **el Día de los Muertos**   b. Las familias se reúnen **para pasar un rato juntos**
c. Los judíos van a la **sinagoga para rezar a su dios**   d. Durante las fiestas hay **desfiles y mercadillos**
e. Cada primavera los **cristianos celebran la Pascua**   f. Tradicionalmente la **gente da regalos a los niños**
g. Es mi fiesta favorita **porque puedo ver a mi familia**   h. El Día de San Valentín **se celebra el 14 de febrero**

11. Gapped translation
a. Durante las fiestas **religiosas**   b. Es mi fiesta **favorita**   c. El Día del **Padre**   d. **Veo** a mis primos
e. Me gustan los **fuegos** artificiales   f. Los **cristianos** van a la **iglesia**   g. **Días** festivos   h. **Pasar** un buen rato
i. Hay **desfiles**   j. Estoy de **vacaciones**   k. Me encanta la **Pascua**

12. Spot and supply the missing words
a. **Recibo** muchos regalos de mi familia   b. Para el Año Nuevo hay **fuegos** artificiales
c. En mi casa celebramos el Día del **Padre**   d. Los musulmanes rezan en las **mezquitas**
e. **Los** amigos y las familias se juntan   f. En la mayoría de las **ciudades** hay desfiles
g. Los **cristianos** celebran la Pascua   h. Durante las fiestas estoy de **vacaciones**   i. Son mis **fiestas** favoritas
j. **Me** encanta reunirme con mi familia   k. El 6 de enero es el Día de los **Reyes** Magos

13. Complete with the missing letters
a. El Día de San Valentín   b. Estas ocasiones especiales   c. En las ciudades hay mercadillos
d. Los judíos celebran Yom Kipur   e. Mi fiesta favorita es la Navidad   f. Me encantan los fuegos artificiales
g. Cada diciembre veo a mi familia   h. Los musulmanes van a la mezquita

14. Anagrams
a. En México celebramos el Día de los Muertos
b. Los cristianos van a la iglesia para rezar
c. Me encantan las fiestas porque estoy de vacaciones
d. La fiesta más importante para los musulmanes es Eid al Fitr
e. En España el Día de la Madre es el primer domingo de mayo
f. El 6 de enero es el Día de los Reyes Magos
g. Las familias y los amigos se reúnen para comer juntos
h. Tradicionalmente los padres dan regalos a sus hijos

15. Complete with an appropriate word
a. La Pascua es la fiesta más **importante** para los cristianos   b. Cada año los hindúes **celebran** Diwali
c. Mis amigos se **reúnen** para pasar un buen **rato** juntos   d. Estas ocasiones son a **menudo** días festivos
e. En la **mayoría** de las ciudades hay desfiles   f. Tradicionalmente la gente **da** regalos a sus parientes
g. Me encanta **ver** los fuegos artificiales   h. Mi fiesta **favorita** es la Navidad
i. Cada año **recibo** muchos regalos de mis padres   j. En mi familia celebramos el **Día** de la Madre
k. Me gustan las fiestas **porque** puedo ver a mis amigos   l. Durante el Yom Kipur los **judíos** van a la sinagoga

16. Guided translation
a. Cada año   b. El Día de los Reyes Magos   c. El Día de la Madre   d. Un buen rato
e. Los fuegos artificiales   f. Rezan a su dios   g. Una comida festiva   h. Los musulmanes   i. En mi casa
j. La gente da   k. Los amigos se reúnen   l. Las familias se juntan   m. Un templo

17. Find the Spanish equivalent in the text
a. Soy española   b. Cada año   c. En casa   d. Celebramos   e. La Navidad   f. Mucho   g. Estoy de vacaciones
h. Veo   i. Buena   j. Juntos   k. Compartimos

18. Complete the translation
On that **day,** after supper, we go to the midnight mass with the **family**. It is the **only** time of the year that I go to
church and I must say that it is **always** a very **beautiful** ceremony.

19. Spot and supply the 10 missing words

Una **semana** después de Navidad, el 31 de diciembre, se celebra la Nochevieja. Para **esta** fiesta normalmente me **junto** con mi familia y algunos amigos. Todos traen **algo** de comer y beber, escuchamos música y **bailamos**. A **medianoche** ponemos la tele y **todos** comemos las **doce** uvas, una por cada **campanada** y nos deseamos un feliz **año** nuevo.

20. Translate into English

a. Christmas Tree   b. Presents/Gifts   c. The most important thing   d. My godmother   e. I appreciate
f. From my parents   g. This special time/season

21. Tick and cross

a. X   b. √   c. √   d. X   e. √   f. X   g. X   h. √   i. X   j. √

22. True, false or not mentioned

a. True   b. True   c. Not mentioned   d. False   e. True   f. True   g. False   h. False   i. True   j. True   k. False

23. Find the Spanish equivalent in the text

a. La fiesta más importante del año   b. Entre enero y febrero   c. Toda mi familia se reúne
d. Comemos comida típica china   e. Para dar la bienvenida a la buena fortuna   f. Colgamos faroles rojos
g. Simbolizan la prosperidad y la buena suerte   h. Mi amiga es musulmana   i. Durante el mes del Ramadán
j. Los musulmanes ayunan durante el día   k. Suelen ir a rezar   l. Voy a regalar flores a mi novia

24. Spot and correct the 8 errors in the translation of paragraph 6

This year, my **girlfriend** and I, we will celebrate together Valentine's Day on the 14th **February**. It is the festival for lovers in **Spain** and some other countries. I am going to give **flowers** to my girlfriend and we are going to go to a restaurant together. **Later/Afterwards**, we will go to the **cinema**. It will be very **romantic**.

25. Word hunt

a. **Día de los enamorados**   b. **Calendar**   c. **Caligrafía**   d. Mi **primo**   e. **Amanecer**   f. **Ayunar**
g. La m**ezquita**

26. Complete with the missing words

a. En **casa** de mis amigos   b. Voy a misa a la i**glesia**   c. Le voy a **regalar** flores
d. Los **judíos** van a la sinagoga   e. Una ceremonia muy b**onita**   f. **Ponemos** la tele y comemos uvas
g. Los m**usulmanes** ayunan   h. Igual que n**osotros** se reúnen   i. Recibo **regalos** de mis padres
j. Después i**remos** al cine   k. Escuchamos música y **bailamos**

27. Guided translation

a. **Voy** a ir al **restaurante**   b. Veo a t**oda** mi **familia**   c. **En casa de mis abuelos**   d. **Voy a misa**
e. Mi **padrino**   f. **Mi madrina**   g. **Nos reunimos**   h. **Es la única época del año**   i. **Regalar flores**
j. **Puedo** d**escansar**   k. **Hasta el atardecer**

28. Translate into Spanish

a. Veo a todos mis parientes en Navidad   b. Cada uno trae algo para comer
c. Siempre hay muchos fuegos artificiales   d. Es la fiesta de los enamorados   e. Será muy romántico
f. Iremos al cine   g. Voy a misa   h. Desde el amanecer hasta el atardecer
i. Voy a ir al restaurante   j. En la mayoría de las ciudades

29. Translate the following paragraphs into Spanish

En mi familia celebramos principalmente la Navidad y la Pascua. La Navidad es mi fiesta favorita porque estoy de vacaciones y veo a todos mis parientes. Por lo general voy a misa y luego nos reunimos/juntamos para una comida festiva. Cada año recibo regalos de mis padres y mi madrina. ¡Es genial! El año pasado fui al mercadillo navideño de mi pueblo y compré chocolate para mis abuelos.

También me gusta el Año Nuevo porque veo a mis amigos y es divertido. La mayor parte del tiempo hay conciertos en el centro de la ciudad y luego fuegos artificiales a medianoche.

En febrero, mi novia y yo celebraremos el Día de San Valentín juntos. Le voy a regalar unas flores y vamos a ir al cine. Será romántico.

30. Guided composition

Free writing

42